Travels with Elly

Reflections on Canada by an
RVer and His Dog

Larry MacDonald, Ph.D.

For information, contact
MSI Press
1760-F Airline Highway, #203
Hollister, CA 95023

Library of Congress Control Number 2019949876

ISBN: 978-1-933455-08-2

DEDICATION

This book is dedicated to Jo van der Veen, a cherished friend whose spirit of adventure and curiosity was with us at every turn. Her best wishes for us came true: "Have an absolutely fascinating journey."

Larry MacDonald, Ph.D.

Contents

Larry MacDonald, Ph.D.

INTRODUCTION

On a balmy afternoon in July, the weather turned ugly—shards of lightning, booming thunder, roiling green and black clouds, and an angry wind that shook our trailer unmercifully. Forecasted tornado warnings in the Edmonton area had me peering through rain-streaked windows at a darkening sky, scanning for dreaded vortexes that would prompt a hasty retreat to our campground's washroom.

A little brown head bunted my leg, chimpanzee-esque eyes expressing concern. "Don't worry," I said, "The odds of dying in a tornado are 20 million to one." *It's the ONE I'm worried about,* she replied, continuing her frantic pacing.

An hour later, sanity returned with mottled grey skies and peaceful prairie breezes. Friedrich Nietzsche, the German philosopher, said it best: "That which does not kill us makes us stronger." That's good—being stronger may have helped us survive even worse weather yet to come, Canada's "Storm of the Century."

In 1960, John Steinbeck traveled across the United States with his poodle, recording his experiences and musings in *Travels with Charley... in Search of America*. Fifty years later, I traveled across Canada with my poodle, also recording my experiences and musings. Our objectives were similar: to gain a better understanding of our respective countries.

The renowned author felt that he had to travel alone because, as he so eloquently stated, "Two or more people disturb the ecologic complex of an area." I briefly discussed this option with my wife, Sandy. During our 38-year relationship, I've learned that there are certain things I can do alone, such as wash windows and mow the yard. But travel across Canada? Not a chance! She succinctly argued that a disturbed ecologic complex was less important than having her along to confirm my observations. Our cat Buster also joined us, as did an unexpected orphan in the latter half of our journey.

When I asked our poodle what she thought about traveling across Canada, she cocked her head slightly left, then further left, her stubby tail rigid like a scimitar. *What a great idea!* Her tail then began wagging like a windshield wiper on fast-forward...*I'll go wherever you go Dad.* She thinks of me as her Dad, having never met her real father, Mel–a regal black poodle, who had won numerous Best-in-Show awards.

Ten years ago, Mel's mate delivered a rainbow of puppies: three white, three black, and three brown. While observing the seven-week-old litter, we focused our attention on a little brown female that explored and roughhoused more than her littermates. According to the breeder, "Browns are clowns," and in her estimation, this puppy was "Pick of the litter." She was not only spirited but also affectionate, licking Sandy's face, snuggling into her neck, and shouting, *PICK ME; PICK ME!* How could we not? Within a few days of trying out a gazillion names, we decided to call her "Elly" after her breeder.

Elly had the requisite conformation to become a show dog having inherited her father's physical characteristics; unfortunately, her lower canine teeth grew so long that they punctured the roof of her mouth, resulting in a severe case of halitosis, which we affectionately called "stinky nose." Although we had the teeth extracted, traces of the noxious smell remained. Over time through many positive associations, we found the familiar odor somewhat appealing. This same principle likely explains why the wife of a dairy farmer who we later visited in Ontario delighted in the tangy scent of cow manure. According to her, "It smells like home." The scent of pig manure on the other hand, she found "disgusting."

When it comes to odours, Elly's keen sense of smell sometimes gets her in trouble. We know she can reliably distinguish between dog feces and deposits from other animals. She'll sniff briefly at a pile of dog-doo and immediately back away; however, let her get a whiff of exotic dreck and a predictable pattern of behaviour unfolds: with eyes focused on the object of interest and nose a measured distance away, she'll prance sideways in a semicircle, first in one direction, then the other. Unless we fortuitously intervene, "Leave it," she'll proceed to the next stages of intimacy with a very deliberate roll, beginning with the side of her head and neck in a caressing motion, then onto her back, wriggling in ecstasy with feet pawing the air. *To me, there's no such word as "gross."*

Once, she rolled gaily on a rotting seal carcass that had washed up on the beach. The stench, and we're talking stinky here, would have made a vulture vomit. *Dad was not amused, waving his arms and hollering a litany of nonsensical words. He wouldn't even let me ride home in the car. So we walked, silently and efficiently, from the beach to our house, then directly into the tub. Several baths later, the deliciously fragrant "bouquet of seal" was but a lingering memory and Dad became his civil self again.*

Steinbeck's Charley also had deformed teeth, which allowed him to say just one word, "Ftt," meaning he had to go outside "to salute a bush or a tree." When Elly has the urge, she'll stare intently at either of us and politely ask, *May I go outside?* If we don't respond, she'll approach the door and shout, *"NOW!"* Once outside and given the appropriate command, "Go pee-pee" or "Go poo-poo," Elly prefers to squat in the woods or in high grass if available, rather than on a manicured lawn. And she never does her business on a walking path, road, or sidewalk. How she learned such appropriately discreet behaviour is a mystery ... certainly not from this Dad. Our friends are always impressed whenever she runs off into the woods and squats behind a bush or tree. *No peeking!*

Aspiring writers are urged to write about things they know. Thus, I write much about Elly, who I know quite well. Her tilted head, pleading eyes, wagging tail, and tentative foot movements all have special meanings that she's taught me over the years. And her thoughts are often more profound than her actions indicate. *I like to think of myself, not as a clown but as a serious observer. I can focus on the antics of a squirrel for hours. Dad thinks I'm obsessed; I consider it being reflective.*

For 30 years, Sandy and I lived in Edmonton, Alberta, where I directed a government program that provided services to persons with intellectual disabilities. Born and raised in Nazareth, Pennsylvania, a three-stoplight town, I immigrated to Canada a few years after college to accept this employment. I have dual citizenship and shared allegiances but choose to live in Canada, a proud yet modest nation respected the world over for its compassion and support of people less fortunate. Since most of my time had been spent in the western provinces, I looked forward to seeing more of my adopted country.

Sandy was born and raised in Ontario and had worked as a special education teacher and social worker. She has a particular gift for interacting with children, seniors, and animals, which facilitated numerous interactions during our journey.

Dad forgot to mention that I was born in Edmonton. My first love, a Bichon Frisé, was also born there. As puppies, Toby and I played together often. One day, he moved far away to Ontario, one of the provinces we plan to visit. I look forward to seeing him again.

Buster is a Rag Doll breed of cat whose defining characteristic is going limp when he's picked up. Having grown up with Elly, the slightly older Buster established himself early on as Alpha and maintained that relationship by a swat or nip on Elly's hindquarters when he decided a playful interlude was over. While Elly was always a great traveler, Buster had some issues, even before our trip began. He occasionally upchucked if a road became too twisty or bumpy for more than 10 or 15 minutes. Buster's problem behaviour stopped suddenly and permanently during our trip, much to our delight. When appropriate, I'll offer my opinion as to why.

After my retirement, we moved to the West Coast of British Columbia and purchased a house. About five years passed. One day, we met a couple that had downsized from their house to a travel trailer without regrets. They were thoroughly enjoying "life on the road" and wished they had done it sooner. After much deliberation, we decided to sell our sticks and bricks and donate everything else that wouldn't fit into a small storage shed. Our new residence consisted of a 38-foot, fifth-wheel trailer—four wheels on the back, the "fifth" being a sturdy pin, which mates to a hitch in the bed of a pick-up truck. Three slideouts provided nearly 500 sq. ft. of living space, considerably less than our 2,400 sq. ft. house but totally adequate for two adults and two animals on the road.

Make no mistake, such a major lifestyle change had some of our friends doubting our sanity. But an equal number were openly envious, wishing their lives could be similarly embellished with more adventure. "Take me with you" typified this group when they found out we were planning an extended road trip. Over the years, we had owned several small motorhomes used primarily for brief camping trips, but this was different—we no longer had a fixed address, permanent neighbours, or the responsibility of maintaining a home. "Nomadic" is how we described our new lifestyle.

Prior to exploring Canada, we took our rig to Arizona the first winter. During this Snowbird experience, I couldn't shake the feeling of being on holidays ... you know, that carefree, happy feeling deep inside that you get when everything is right with the world. Being on holidays seems to bring out the excited and curious child within. I've gotten this feeling many times during my adult life while holidaying in the Caribbean, South Pacific, and other exotic places. But it always faded when the holiday was over and life got back to ordinary. This time, however, I wasn't going back to ordinary. George Bernard Shaw once remarked, "A perpetual holiday is a good working definition of Hell." Personally, I would have substituted Heaven for Hell.

In RV (Recreational Vehicle) vernacular, we're called "Full-Timers," referring to the large and growing number of folks who live in their rigs. Sandy's modesty prompts her to inform everyone who admires our large, well-appointed trailer: "It's our home." This occurred so often during our journey that I was tempted to attach a sign, WE LIVE HERE FULL TIME!

Fifty years ago, recreational vehicles were less common, providing a measure of novelty to Steinbeck's camper, which he affectionately named "Rocinante" after Don Quixote's horse. Following his lead, we also named our rig. Since our truck carried the load, we named it "Tenzing" after the Sherpa employed by Sir Edmund Hillary. Our trailer we named "Barouche," after an elegant four-wheel carriage popular in the 1800's. Clever names I thought, but seldom used in our ordinary conversations—we typically referred to them as the truck and the trailer.

After purchasing our rig, my insurance agent informed me that I would require a Heavy Trailer Endorsement to pull a trailer over 10,000 pounds. Ours was half again that heavy. Obtaining this endorsement involved a written test, followed by a drive-about under the critical eye of an Examiner. No worries. Down I went to the licensing office for the written —which I promptly flunked, a humbling experience for someone with a Ph.D. who had been driving nearly half a century. A few days later, after perusing the information booklet that I should have read in the first place, I proudly passed the written and subsequently the drive-about, validating my insurance. Interestingly, people who drive large motorhomes do not currently require any special testing in Canada. Why the distinction between these behemoth cruisers and towed trailers is beyond me, considering their similar potential for causing major damage on our roadways.

Steinbeck took three months to cover 10,000 miles, often driving relentlessly day and night. We traveled at a more leisurely pace, taking ten months to cover half that distance. Seldom did we drive more than three hours at a stretch. His small truck-camper allowed forays onto back roads and pastures, getting him close to the sights and smells of rural America. Our much larger rig precluded excursions on unfamiliar side roads. Nevertheless, we did occasionally access rural Canada by unhooking the trailer and bouncing down dirt roads in the truck.

Our plan was to travel across Canada, observe surroundings, chat with locals, and identify characteristics that define each Province as well as Canadians in general. Our approach, different from Steinbeck's, included visits to museums, monuments, and various other tourist attractions. Steinbeck felt that "stupendous works of man or nature," such as Yellowstone National Park, are "no more representative of America than Disneyland." I, on the other hand, would argue that such natural wonders define a country's geographic diversity, while stupendous man-made objects often reflect a region's historical or cultural identity. Thus, our palette of topics ranged from the first settlement and prettiest town to the greatest hero and most devastating shipwreck in Canada. And of course, we included activities that might interest our dear Miss Elly.

We had legitimate concerns about surviving a Canadian winter in a poorly insulated trailer. Annual temperatures in Canada can range anywhere from -40 to +40 degrees Celsius. Since the minus signs are associated with snow, icy roads, wind chill, and runny noses, the prudent thing to do would be to break the trip into two parts. During the first four months, July to October, we would travel from British Columbia to Ontario. From there, like migrating geese, we would head south to spend the winter in Florida. Returning in the spring, we would spend the next six months traveling from Ontario to Newfoundland.

BRITISH COLUMBIA

1

"Log for the future—stop clear cutting"
Handmade sign in Nelson

Many Canadians we met during our journey were not quite sure where our hometown of Powell River is located. "Are you on Vancouver Island?" they would ask. "No, but we can see Vancouver Island across the Strait of Georgia. We're on the mainland two ferry rides north of Vancouver." Plans are in the works for building a road from Vancouver, but until that happens, Powell River will remain somewhat remote. The town was established in 1910 to sustain a lumber mill that once employed over 2000 people. When we left in 2009, the town had become a city with 15,000 residents and a tenuously surviving paper mill employing less than 400. Powell River has become more of a retirement haven, especially for those who enjoy outdoor activities such as hiking, biking, boating, and fishing. The pace is slow, people are friendly, and the climate is moderate, making it a desirable place to call home. We still do, even though we're gone most of the time. After returning from Arizona, we spent a couple of months at a local campground, just long enough to reconnect with friends before setting off on our big adventure.

Our campsite in Powell River, British Columbia prior to departure

A well-worn proverb states that every journey, no matter how long, begins with a single step. We began ours by walking knee deep into the Georgia Strait, pumping our fists excitedly as if the Canucks had just won the Stanley Cup. As every Canadian male over the age of four knows, the term "Canucks" in this context refers to the Vancouver ice hockey team. It also refers to Canadians en-mass, generally in an affectionate way. Elly joined us by walking in chest deep, emphatically stating, *This is quite far enough in my studied opinion.* I'll elaborate on the rationale for this comment later in our journey.

Our departure date of July 1 coincided with Canada Day, a statutory holiday for citizens to celebrate the birth of Canada. We would learn the details of this birthing process during our visit to Prince Edward Island, the province where it all started 142 years ago. In spite of the anticipated heavy traffic, we chose to join the masses headed to the ferry terminal south of the city. About 15 minutes along a twisty stretch of highway, Buster reliably reviewed his breakfast in a towel we kept handy for such emergencies.

Along this same stretch, a disturbing number of stumps, discarded saplings, and logging tracks extend down to the highway. Vast areas of such clear-cutting are prominent along many of BC's highways and much controversy exists between logging companies and environmentalists. John Vaillant in **The Golden Spruce** describes the history of the logging industry in BC, including its destructive practice of indiscriminate clear-cutting.

The main character Grant Hadwin was initially a logger but converted to a staunch environmentalist, and thereafter became frustrated with his futile attempts to convince political figures and logging companies to change their ways. Unfortunately, his misguided strategy to shed attention on the plight of BC forests was to cut down an ancient and rare golden spruce in the Queen Charlotte Islands (now called Haida Gwaii) that was revered by the Haida Indians. He was suspected of doing so and in fact admitted it, but disappeared, presumed drowned, before coming to trial for this grievous but profoundly premeditated act.

I asked Elly what she thought about this practice of clear-cutting forests. *Like most of my friends, I much prefer to walk in a forest, than in a field of stumps.* A quote from Henry David Thoreau came to mind: "Thank God, they cannot cut down the clouds."

The decreasing demand for lumber worldwide has decimated the lumber industry in BC with more mills closing or downsizing each year. Another related concern is the widespread destruction of forests by the mountain pine beetle. This rapidly spreading insect lays its eggs under the bark of pine trees. After hatching, the larvae feed on the trees, killing them within a year. Throughout the province, stands of dead pine present as red and grey splotches on otherwise verdant mountainsides, providing a potential source of fuel for forest fires. Only a stretch of extremely cold weather can kill this beetle, but with global warming on the rise, this outcome is unlikely in the foreseeable future. Reportedly, in just a few years pine beetles will have destroyed most of the marketable pine in BC — a dismal picture for those whose livelihoods depend on forestry.

After a one-ferry wait, we departed on a short but scenic passage from the upper to the lower Sunshine Coast. Pristine mountains, islands, bays, and a substantial waterfall (if you know where to look) provide a sampling of BC's natural beauty. A short drive later, we arrived at the seaside village of Davis Bay where we had rented a house during our first year on the coast. With the trailer parked in our former neighbour's driveway, we spent several days visiting friends, including our beloved Jo, a spry 92 year-old to whom this book is dedicated. She was originally going to join us for the BC portion of our trip but suffered a minor heart attack, just weeks before our departure. Having traveled the world, Jo looked forward to the adventure of being on the road. Her compassion, boundless energy, wit, and willingness to "try everything at least once" would have made each day a measure fuller for Sandy and me. Regrettably, it was not to be. Shortly after we left, Jo sold her house and moved into a care residence. We still felt her presence and kept in touch with phone calls and postcards from various ports of call.

Jo, pursuing one of her many passions

A short distance south, we boarded another ferry that took us to Horseshoe Bay on the threshold of Vancouver. Bordered by the majestic Coast Mountain Range and the Strait of Georgia, Vancouver was voted by CBC "the most beautiful city in Canada." Unfortunately, on this day (and likely most days) the frenetic pace of traffic tarnished its beauty. Everyone seemed to be in a hurry, cutting in and out like desperate couriers on piece-rate. When pulling a large trailer such as ours, sufficient stopping distance is required in the event of an emergency stop. Five seconds is the recommended time between a vehicle ahead passing a point and me passing the same point. Inevitably, whenever I slowed down to provide that margin of safety, another hurried driver seized the vacant piece of highway. Little wonder I needed an adult beverage when we finally arrived at our campground.

Having explored Vancouver many times previously, we stayed just two days at an outlying RV park, allowing time for a visit with a previous work colleague. Her husband professes to make the best martini in the land so whenever we get together, the competitive juices and the gin start flowing. I call mine a "Titanic" because of its large size and judicious amount of ice chips, with three olives of course. By evening's end, he considered himself "unsinkable." His teetotalling wife took the helm when they departed to ensure they didn't hit any icebergs on their way home.

Every city, regardless of size, has both good and bad features. Vancouver, Canada's third largest city, has an abundance of cultural and recreational activities: museums, concerts, street festivals, boating, skiing, swimming, hiking, and endless parks, shopping, and eateries. On the other hand, besides its snarling traffic, Vancouver has a major slum, Downtown East Side, with its share of unsavoury characters, drug trafficking, and crime. By comparison, a small city like Powell River doesn't have as many cultural opportunities as Vancouver; nor does it have as many social problems. Less good, less bad is more desirable in my opinion, which leads me to favour small-town living.

Decisions about where to live are typically based on lifestyle demands. If you need a job to maintain a certain lifestyle and that job is only available in a big city, that's where you'll live, just as we lived in Edmonton for 30 years. After retiring, material needs often become less important, allowing more options on where to call home. Even then, most retirees continue to live where they worked because of familiarity and social networks. A minority, like us, move on.

Continuing east on the Trans-Canada Highway, our next stop was a campground near Bridal Falls. We spent a few days enjoying walks to the falls and visiting nearby Harrison Hot Springs, where a world-renowned sandcastle-building competition is held each year. We were early for that event but did take a relaxing walk around the lake. Elly enjoyed fetching sticks thrown into the water until they floated outside of her comfort zone.

No amount of verbal encouragement would entice her to retrieve a stick beyond chest high water. *Why should I risk drowning for a lousy stick when there's a whole bunch more on the beach?* How could I argue with that logic? Elly had never learned to swim and a purebred heritage could not override her skill deficit. Whenever she gets in deep water, she tries to touch bottom with her hind paws, her little head bobbing up and down until she reaches land – a very inefficient doggy paddle. *Nonsense, I consider my swimming style to be "vertically oriented" rather than "inefficient."*

In Germany, where poodles originated, hunters used this breed to retrieve slain game birds that ended up in the water. The distinctive patches of hair on their chest and legs were intended to keep their vitals and joints warm, while the remainder of their body was shaved to make them lighter and faster swimmers. Today, poodle show-dogs continue to display these now nonfunctional pom-poms and shaved body parts. Elly's natural cut and brown colour are so un-poodle-like, that very few people could identify her breed. "Is she a Portuguese water dog? Goldendoodle? Labradoodle?" Again and again, we'd reply, "No, she's a Standard Poodle." In Newfoundland, one tourist even asked, "Is she a Newfie?" which is a black dog about the size of a lowland gorilla. Since Elly only weighs 40 pounds, I assumed the visitor was desperately hoping to meet a local breed.

On the next leg to Kamloops, we continued along the Fraser River instead of taking the more direct Coquahalla Highway. Stopping briefly at Hell's Gate, we marveled at the volume and turbulence of water gushing through the narrow canyon. Raft tours continue to be offered to willing passengers. When we asked Elly if she wanted to go rafting, she ran back to the truck!

As we proceeded northward, the lush mountainous terrain gave way to a more barren landscape with interesting names like Gold Rush Trail, Jackass Mountain, and The Nipple. I could visualize a gold prospector leading his donkey on a mountain trail, but the derivation of The Nipple eluded me. Trust me, I looked expectantly, but never saw anything resembling a nipple.

Just north of the town of Spence's Bridge, we were forced to stop in a seemingly endless line of traffic. A motorcyclist who had turned around informed us that an accident had occurred several kilometres ahead and the police were conducting an investigation. After waiting impatiently for what seemed like an hour, in reality probably 15 minutes, I conjured up a plan to turn around and take an alternate route to intersect the Coquahalla Highway. Obviously, turning around the equivalent of a semi-truck on a two-lane road can be problematic. However, I noticed a pullout about a half-kilometre ahead on the left side. If I could just get a couple of drivers to move, I could use the pullout and back into their space. Cautiously edging out of line, much to Sandy's chagrin, I drove on the wrong side of the road to the pullout. While I waited, Sandy asked the two drivers if they would temporarily move aside. Both graciously obliged and after some careful maneuvering to the applause of a bored audience, we were headed in the opposite direction.

Sometimes, unplanned diversions result in pleasant outcomes. Feeling a wee-bit peckish, we pulled over at a small roadside restaurant operated by a delightful young couple who prided themselves on serving wholesome, organic, farm-fresh foods. Our entire meal – scrambled eggs, salads with edible flowers, lattes, and freshly baked raspberry cream tarts – was superb. Surprisingly, with the exception of two bikers, no one else was there. I suggested they put up a few signs on both sides of the highway, each advertising one of their food items like the lattes and raspberry cream tarts. The lady lamented, almost apologetically, "We had a sign but a snowplow knocked it down last winter." Apparently, marketing and preparing gourmet meals are two distinct skill sets that don't always coexist. We wished them well and continued on to Merritt.

The Coquahalla is a 200 kilometre four-lane highway providing breathtaking views of mountains and valleys while shortening driving times between central BC and the lower mainland. Its long, steep uphill grades were handled easily by our truck with its powerful diesel engine and factory tow package designed to maintain the automatic transmission in several lower gears. To retard downhill speeds, the engine's compression known as a "Jake Brake" complemented the truck and trailer's disk brakes. An hour north of Merritt, the "Coke" empties onto the Trans-Canada, which immediately descends from a mountaintop to the valley floor over several kilometres. Periodic emergency "run outs" with extensive crushed rock are available in the event of break failure. I've often been tempted to use one, just to see how effective they are, but Sandy insisted, "Not this trip!"

The air became noticeably warmer and drier the lower we descended until we reached our campground beside the Thompson River, where cooler breezes prevailed. When passing through this sprawling city on previous trips between Edmonton and the coast, we'd sometimes book into a motel for a night before setting off again. On those occasions, I always considered its barren hills and desert-like environment to be somewhat inhospitable. However, after spending a few days here, I felt compelled to reassess these superficial impressions.

After setting up the trailer, we visited a couple we had met in Arizona during the previous winter. Their mountainside condo overlooked an outstanding multi-level golf course, which my friend encouraged me to play – not a hard sell. The next day, we all drove up to a four-season resort on

Todd Mountain. Dirt bikers hurtled down bare ski slopes, golfers ambled about on lush fairways, and joyful visitors dined on outdoor patios. A high level of youthful energy permeated the village, most notably in several of the bistros. After an early dinner, we quietly departed and returned to the trailer to play Bid Euchre, a card game that only a handful of Canadians, including most of Sandy's relatives, play.

On our final day, we toured the town and dined at a couple of great restaurants. Everyone—vendors, waiters, and people on the street—was very friendly. By the end of our visit, we could more fully appreciate why our friends loved living here. The lesson learned was that the heart and soul of a city, as with a lover, can best be revealed by prolonged intimacy. That being the case, we agreed there would be no one-night stands for us during out travels across Canada.

Our next stop was an Okanogan Valley campground, located on the eastern shore of Swan Lake. Gigantic willows provided shade and ambiance while ducks and geese cavorted about in shallow enclaves. Over the next four days, we got reacquainted with a former colleague of mine, who had moved from Edmonton to Vernon to accept a position in our mutual field of mental disabilities. Four days turned into six due to some recent forest fires further down the Valley where we had planned to camp next.

During our passage through BC, several hundred fires raged partly due to prolonged periods of hot, dry weather. Fires kill the pine-beetle infestations but they also threaten homes, force evacuations, and provide Nature's destructive alternative to clear cutting.

With the wind blowing in our direction, the Valley became laden with acrid smoke, reminiscent of the devastating fires of 2003 near this same area. During that inferno, hundreds of square kilometres of forests were destroyed while hundreds of residents lost their homes.

Emergency road closures necessitated taking an alternate route east to Nakusp, a small community in the West Kootenays. Along the way, we boarded a ferry, which took us across Lower Arrow Lake. The ride was free, as it is on all 14 interior ferries operated by the Ministry of Transportation.

Not so on the coast. BC Ferries, a Crown Corporation, charges for vehicles and passengers ... and it's not cheap. The recent fee for transporting our rig from Powell River to Vancouver was about $200. Many people who must rely on ferry travel get annoyed at the high fees, arguing that ferries are part of the highway system and thus should be funded through tax dollars. They reference the free interior ferries to make their point. So where's the logic here, paying for some ferries and not others? If anyone asks, which I doubt they will, I would recommend placing a referendum on the next provincial ballot to give British Columbians a choice regarding this issue.

My vote is "yes" to free ferries.

This serendipitous diversion into the West Kootenays exposed us to yet another slice of a very large scenic pie, worthy of its license-plate slogan, "Beautiful BC." Our campsite was situated on a grassy plane leading down to Summit Lake, back-dropped by verdant mountains. Fishermen in small boats trolled back and forth on pristine water, catching the occasional trout and whitefish. Some campers took advantage of the sunshine, soaking up rays on the sandy beach; others threw horseshoes, while still others played a joyous game of bocce ball. Fun and relaxation seemed to be the order of the day. Surprisingly, in spite of many fires in the province, smoke curled skyward from several campsites.

I walked Elly onto a dock where long-legged spiders shuttled erratically on the water's sheened surface. She stretched her neck as low as possible over the edge mesmerized by these strange denizens.

Elly, keeping a watchful eye on water striders

As I watched her staring into the water for ten minutes, I thought dogs are so easily amused. Then I realized I was watching her staring into the water! Finally, I called, "Come on Elly, it's time to go."

Ahh, do we have to?

"Yes," I fibbed, "But we'll come back tomorrow." I fibbed again.

I wish Dad could live in the moment like I do. He's always in a hurry to go someplace, usually when I'm just starting to have fun.

Elly's right, I get a restless feeling whenever I'm in one place too long; going elsewhere seems to set me at ease. Somewhere in my Scottish lineage, I suspect one of my ancestors married a gypsy.

Our camping neighbours had only planned to stay one night, but were nearing the end of their second week. We also extended our stay in this idyllic spot for a few more days, giving us an opportunity to visit Sandy's cousin who lived a half-hour south in Silverton.

Sandy hadn't seen Shelly in 20 years so their reunion was quite eventful with lots of hugs, laughter, and a few tears. Two years ago, Shelly's partner Doug was a burly construction worker when he tumbled backward down a flight of stairs, changing his life in an instant. Waking up in hospital with a crushed spinal cord, his new status of "incomplete quadriplegic" meant that he had limited use of his arms and legs. As well, both hands were locked in a claw position. After two years of rehab, he had just started learning to operate a computer using a voice-recognition program, hoping to obtain a related job.

In a private moment, Doug and I discussed his situation in comparison to the late Christopher Reeves, a "complete quadriplegic" who was only able to perform tasks by sipping and puffing on an air tube. Doug admitted that, although initially angry and feeling pitiful, he was grateful that he could do so much more than Christopher and was happy with his rate of improvement—from immobile to taking baby steps, using a walker and Shelly for support. His greatest annoyance was that he couldn't scratch his head when it itched. Oh boy! I vowed to never again complain of my slight limp, the result of a snow skiing accident. I recall reading somewhere that if we all bundled our troubles, threw them in the centre of a room, and were asked to choose a bundle, we might well choose our own.

The following day, we again met Shelly and one of her girl friends in nearby New Denver. While walking about town, they gave us a running commentary of the town's use as an internment camp for over 1500 Japanese Canadians who had previously lived on the BC coast at the outbreak of WWII. These citizens were rounded up and forced to live in small clapboard shacks, many of which still line the residential streets. A museum houses artifacts and stories of these sad times. Shamefully, over 22,000 Canadians of Japanese heritage were detained in such camps across Canada. Desperate times demand desperate measures; but in a civilized society, citizens should be judged by their individual actions, not by their ancestral affiliations.

I asked Shelly's friend, who had previously lived near Vancouver, why she chose New Denver to settle down. After a thoughtful pause, she replied, " Well, first of all, look at the scenery. And second, if there were ever a Holocaust, I would be totally self-sufficient here in the Valley. I grow and raise everything needed for survival." I totally agreed with the scenery part and jotted down her address in the event of a Holocaust.

With fond farewells, we headed south overlooking magnificent Slocan Lake for nearly an hour. Arriving at the small town of Nelson was like stepping back in time a hundred years. From 1890 through 1910, various commercial buildings were constructed here with decorative facades, including bracketed cornices, arched windows, and towers. An Architectural Heritage Tour identifies over two-dozen such buildings within the downtown core, all maintained in their original state.

After the Tour, we visited art galleries, funky shops, a sidewalk café, and a lakeside park with a labyrinth, "IF WALKED IN SILENCE RESULTS IN ENLIGHTENMENT." I wondered if my reluctance to walk its entirety would result in at least partial enlightenment!

From Nelson, we crossed Kootenay Lake on another free ferry and stayed near a local golf course that Sandy encouraged me to play while she moseyed through the artisan shops of Crawford Bay. My playing partners started out friendly enough but became less so as their games deteriorated. In fairness, an excess of bubbly may have contributed to losing their tempers, or better put, finding their tempers. Throwing clubs and taking unnecessary divots during practice swings presumably assuaged their anger. They obviously adhered to the axiom: Life is not serious; GOLF is serious. I wanted to ask, "Hey guys, will it really matter next week what you score today?" But a sense of self-preservation prevailed. I'm not a great golfer, but rather than get upset over some errant shots, I mentally repeat: "It's only a game. It's only a game." I use that mantra quite often!

Following the shoreline of Kootenay Lake, we headed south on the twistiest stretch of road since the beginning of our trip. Buster threw up reliably after 15 minutes, but just once during more than an hour of weaving. We didn't know it at the time, but that would be his last adverse reaction to curvy roads. I assumed that prolonged exposure to curves allowed Buster to relax instead of getting anxious.

In psychology, a similar outcome occurs when Implosive Therapy is used to cure phobias. If a patient has an irrational fear, for example of spiders, treatment involves the psychologist "imploding" or flooding the person with images of spiders crawling on their arms and legs, or even in their ears and mouth. Prolonged exposure to these worst-case scenarios results in a lessening of anxiety as the person learns that no adverse consequences follow. Had I known that a cure for Buster's malady was simply prolonged exposure to curvy roads, I would have driven that shoreline years ago.

Our destination was St. Eugene Casino near Cranbrook. Occasionally, unless weather conditions required the use of our heater or air conditioner, we sought out alternatives to paid camping. Our favourite was Casino parking lots, which were only free if we managed to stay out of the Casino! Lavish buffets were usually reasonably priced as an incentive to come in, eat, and play. Other free overnight options included parking lots at movie theatres, churches, fairgrounds, box stores, and truck stops as well as driveways of friends and family.

The casino building, built in 1910, had originally been used as a Residential School for thousands of Indian children from the surrounding areas, another shameful example of the Canadian government's discriminatory practices. Later in Manitoba, we would hear heartbreaking stories from a native woman who had actually attended one such school in that province. Residential Schools closed in 1970 when government policy changed to encourage public education for native children. The First Nation bands here in BC turned the tarnished icon into a destination resort, employing 250 people, 25% from First Nations.

At the time of our visit, this was the only project in Canada where an Indian Residential School had been converted into a profitable business enterprise, a credit to the participating native bands. I contributed to their coffers by playing a round on their beautiful golf course, but managed to stay out of the Casino. We left the next morning, Alberta bound.

Our final stretch of highway in BC took us through Sparwood where we stopped briefly to view the "Largest Truck in the World," a massive yellow dump truck once used in the local coal mines. To give some idea of its size, my nearly six-foot frame reached only to the centre of the front tire.

Author in Sparwood, British Columbia

Canadians seem to have a penchant for building huge icons, most of which represent some cultural or industrial aspect of a community. Alberta alone is home to the largest Easter egg, largest perogy, largest sausage, and largest shopping centre in Canada. But the granddaddy of all things man-made is Alberta's oil-sands project, which I planned to visit during our travels through that province.

Larry MacDonald, Ph.D.

2

ALBERTA

*"If we hope to preserve our way of life, the first thing we must do is redis-
cover our respect for the land, the water, and the entire natural world.
And if we do manage to regain that respect, then we must make sure that
human beings never lose it again."*

**Quote from the late, The Honourable Dr. Lois E. Hole, displayed on a
plaque at the Lois Hole Centennial Provincial Park in St. Albert**

Shortly after crossing the border, we entered Crowsnest Pass, site
of the devastating Frank Slide. In the early morning of April 29, 1903, a
mountainside came thundering down in the darkness, burying most of the
town of Frank and killing 90 people, the highest death toll from any slide in
Canada. Massive boulders, remnants of the slide, remain piled 30-metres
high on both sides of the road.

An Interpretation Centre provides personal stories of survivors and
dynamic, hands-on educational programs. To forewarn residents and prevent such a tragedy in the future, the government has established a state-
of-the-art monitoring system on the remaining mountain that can measure movements as small as the thickness of a penny.

Further east, a cadre of giant propellers turned stealthy in the breeze,
generating electricity for surrounding communities. This wind-turbine
farm is ideally situated to take advantage of strong westerly winds that funnel through the mountain pass. Reportedly, environmentalists have raised
concerns over its aesthetic impact, sound pollution, and deadly effects on

migratory birds. Unfortunately, as long as consumers require energy, some degradation of the environment appears to be inevitable, barring the discovery of alternative forms of clean energy. Perhaps the self-sustaining lifestyle of Shelly's friend in the Kootenays is indeed the solution for a cleaner, greener Canada. In fact, David Hadwin outlined a similar although somewhat more radical strategy shortly before felling the golden spruce:

"Dismantle society as we know it, abolish all currency and religion, and remove all men from power. Replace the status quo with small, agrarian villages run by women and restricted to pre-industrial technology. The sole purpose of these matriarchal communities would be to repair the damage wrought by the past two thousand years of male-dominated civilization."

Sandy thought it was worth a try. I wondered if living in a trailer in an agrarian village would diminish that feeling of being on holidays!

Would not the world be a better place if each of us made just one small sacrifice to reduce our carbon footprint? Sandy and I have occasionally been asked how we justify our nomadic lifestyle from an environmental standpoint. Our typical response compares our energy usage now to when we lived in a house. Fewer materials are required to build a trailer than a house, less fuel is required to heat or cool it, and less energy-wasting devices, such as lawn mowers and snow blowers, are required to maintain it. Our truck uses diesel fuel instead of gasoline, which requires less energy to process, and our annual mileage is about the same as the combined mileage of our previous two cars. We also use our bicycles for short trips when in a campground.

What hasn't changed is our penchant to recycle and to not buy new clothing and appliances if older items are still serviceable. We take cloth shopping bags into grocery stores to reduce the need for plastic bags, and we buy Canadian, preferably local, rather than imports, when possible. Could we do more? Certainly—and we will when the Holocaust occurs, prompting our move to New Denver!

Several things about Alberta are noticeably different from British Columbia. First, the sky is bluer, almost navy, and the small white cumulous clouds are flatter, as if their bottoms have been shaved off.

Second, partially accounting for the stratified clouds, the land is mostly flat toward the east, a feature we never noticed when we lived here. Only after being surrounded by mountains for five years did this prairieness become evident.

Third, houseflies are much more prevalent in Alberta. On the coast, we can leave our doors and windows open and only the occasional insect enters. At our southern Alberta campground, flies zoomed in every time the door opened. Perhaps the expansive herds of cows we saw along Alberta's highways had something to do with the large numbers of flies.

Sandy, who had spent many summers on her Uncle's dairy farm, regularly reminded me about the difference between male and female cattle. To me, all cattle are cows. To her, only females are "cows." Males have other names like bulls or steers. She's correct, of course, but it doesn't matter: they both attract flies, and that's the point here. Whenever Buster spotted a fly in the trailer, he shifted into attack mode, riveting on and stalking the doomed insect until he knocked it out of the air and into his mouth with a couple of swift whacks. Except for the fly, it was a win-win situation: Buster got his exercise and protein and we had one less fly to shoo.

Sandy's sister Margot and her husband Randy invited us to park in their driveway during our visit to Calgary. For the next week, we did mostly family things, including a picnic along the Elbow River in honour of their mom's birthday.

When we got to the picnic site, I was pleasantly surprised with the diversity of cultural groups: Hispanic, East Indians, Aboriginals, Afro-Americans, and Italians interspersed with white Anglo-Saxons. Canada has a tradition of being a melting pot of cultures, another reason I choose to live here. In my opinion, diversity produces strength in nationalities just as it does in gene pools. Geneticists call it "heterogeneity" and encourage crossbreeding to reduce the incidence of traits harmful to offspring. For example, in-breeding of show dogs can lead to hip dysplasia, breathing problems, tumors, and a host of other undesirable traits. In terms of nationalities, Canada supports policies that are accepting of people from other countries, ultimately increasing the strength of its cultural fabric.

Margot is a superb cook and we thoroughly appreciated her home-cooked meals, followed by some friendly games of Bid-Euchre. Randy and I golfed twice and each time, a rare event occurred. A lady in our foursome made her first hole-in-one; the next day Randy made his first in 50 years of serious golfing. To put this event into perspective, some pro golfers who play almost every day have never gotten a hole-in-one in tournament play. Witnessing two in two days—unbelievable! Since Randy and I have both had a hole-in-one, we made a friendly wager of $100 for whoever gets another first, with credible witnesses of course.

A 3-hour drive north to Edmonton took us through prime farm and ranch land with herds of cows on both sides of the highway. Some may have been males, but even Sandy couldn't tell at highway speeds. Dogs reportedly have an average vocabulary of about 200 words. Elly, we'd like to think, is above average. She definitely knows the word "cows." Whenever we said, "Look at the cows" she'd sit bolt upright in the back seat, jerking her head back and forth until she saw one. She then focused on another, and another, until the herd was gone. She did the same when we said, "Look at the horses." I should mention that she behaved remarkably similar when we said, "Look at the hay bales," so we've not sure she was capturing the essence of farm animals. *Of course I know a hay bale from a cow; you can't get milk from a hay bale!*

Sandy and I had the comfortable feeling of returning "home" as we passed familiar landmarks driving to our campsite in St. Albert, a bedroom community of Edmonton. We allocated a month to visit friends, some of whom we hadn't seen since our departure six years ago. Time passed quickly. I golfed a fair bit. Sandy and Elly visited friends, both human and canine. One day, Elly romped through a park with some of her old buddies.

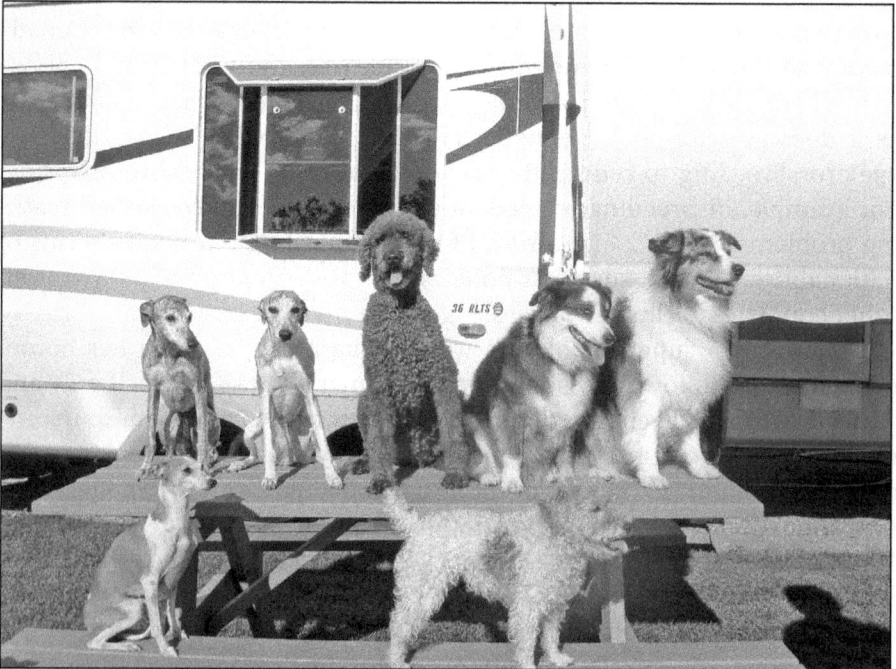

Elly with friends in Edmonton, Alberta

On another day, we walked Elly into our old condo complex, and in spite of being gone for half her life, she led us straight to our unit. She also stared through the fence at a neighbour's condo where a Siberian Husky had lived. When we said, "It's time to leave," she looked puzzled. *You mean we're not going inside?*

We were repeatedly awed by Elly's memory for early events in her life. When we visited her breeder, she wiggled and smiled like a kid in a candy store. We had only seen her smile twice before, both times with her breeder. *I love you Elly.* "I love you too Elly," replied the breeder.

Edmonton is the Capitol City of Alberta, close in size to Calgary— about a million people. A friendly rivalry exists between their football and hockey teams. Both cities have expanded rapidly over the past ten years, partly to support the oil-sands projects in northern and central Alberta, the largest known deposit of oil sands in the world.

Because of its significance economically, politically, and environmentally, I had to see it for myself. Sandy remained at the campground with the critters, allowing me the opportunity to visit for a couple of days.

Fort McMurray, 400 kilometres north of Edmonton, serves as the main staging area for projects in the Athabasca Oil Sands. Projects are also underway in the Peace River and Cold Lake areas.

Combined, the Oil Sands covers 140,000 square kilometres, nearly a quarter of the size of Alberta and slightly smaller than the state of Florida. Since the 1960's, every major oil company has staked a claim to extract this oil, making this also the world's largest construction project.

A friend in Edmonton suggested I drive up midweek to avoid heavy traffic occurring after shift changes on Thursdays and Sundays. Route 63, a two-lane, 150-kilometre highway terminating in Fort McMurray, had acquired the infamous label "Highway of Death." During a four-year period between 2001 and 2005, a thousand accidents occurred on this stretch, killing 25 people and injuring 300 more. I could easily see why: a procession of tanker trucks and semi-trailers, some driving slowly with oversized loads, were interspersed with cars and vans driven mostly by employees intent on leaving or arriving back at Fort Mac in a hurry.

Amazed at the number of trucks using the highway, I decided to take a survey of 100 vehicles heading south. During the next half-hour, I counted almost twice as many trucks as cars: 64 to 34 with one bus and one motorcycle. Not only did the survey relieve boredom, the mental gymnastics of classifying vehicles kept me from passing recklessly.

Conspicuously absent on this highway were strategically located Passing Zone signs to inform motorists of upcoming safe-passing lanes. Later in our journey on a two-lane highway in Northern Ontario, I noticed such signs, usually at 10, 5, and 2 kilometres before the passing lanes. Would not the placement of such signs here deter drivers from passing on a dangerous stretch of road, knowing that a passing lane would soon be available? I think so, with one caveat: the placement of Passing Zone signs at 10 kilometres sends the wrong message to impatient drivers—that they have a long time to wait before they can get around that slowpoke in front of them.

Sandy often comments that I am obsessed with signage. "Obsessed" is a word I reserve for Elly; however, I do occasionally get irate at the inappropriate usage (or non-usage) of signs. The need for Passing Zone signs on Route 63 is just one of many examples I felt compelled to address as we traveled across Canada.

Pulling into town mid-afternoon, I found myself in a massive traffic jam. Fort Mac has only 80,000 residents, but another 50,000 workers are employed at the various Projects. A bus driver I later spoke with commented: "The streets and highways are woefully inadequate to handle the massive amounts of traffic."

I agreed, having been stuck in traffic for a half-hour trying to make my way to a motel.

I had hoped to get a tour of a Project but the Visitor Centre Host said that they stopped giving them a week ago. She suggested an aerial tour but the price of $180 was prohibitive for my budget since I had already paid that much for a motel room. Prices were hugely inflated here; my motel room was at least twice what I would have paid in Edmonton.

I decided to follow the advice of my Edmonton friend, continuing north another 50 kilometres to the end of the paved road. This drive allowed me to observe the sheer size of these Projects.

In a word, they are mind-boggling. Extensive open-pit mines have gigantic shovels and dump trucks transferring oil-impregnated sand and rock to massive conveyer belts or crusher units, and onward to huge processing complexes. Rows of stacks belch smoke into the air, obscuring the horizon. Think big. Now think monstrous. One shovel can scoop up 100 tons of earth, equivalent in weight to 12 elephants. Three scoops can fill one three-story-high truck.

Monster scoop in Fort McMurray, Alberta

Four hundred buses are required to transport workers between their camps, the city, and the Project sites. The camps, which can hold up to 2,500 workers, look like single-wide trailers stacked three high covering areas as large as a city block. I just kept shaking my head in disbelief at the sheer size and busyness of it all.

Downwind of some open-pit mines, the distinct smell of oil permeated the air, likely the "smell of money" for employees. I asked a lady who had lived in Fort McMurray all of her 35 years, "Why do you live here?"

She said, "My friends and family are all here, and everyone is so friendly."

She didn't notice any difference in the air quality between here and other cities such as Edmonton. Unfortunately, our bodies often adapt to low-level noxious events until irreparable damage occurs; then, it's too late. Reportedly, downstream of Projects along the adjacent Athabasca River, Aboriginals are experiencing such irreparable damage in the form of rare cancers.

At one of the camps, I spoke to a worker who said he hoped to leave as soon as he retires. When I asked how long he had worked in the Oil Sands, he said, "25 years. I plan to work another five to receive a full pension; then I'm outa here." Although his doctor suggested that he might experience health problems from continuous exposure to toxic fumes, his six-figure salary forced him to stick it out.

Returning to the "Fort," I drove by some tailing ponds that contained discarded water with traces of oil. These tailing ponds cover 176 square kilometres and can be seen from outer space. Scarecrows and periodic shotgun blasts intended to scare birds away are not always successful. The ill-fated birds that land in these ponds become contaminated with oil and die, either nearby or further along their migration routes. When I asked a worker about it, he flippantly replied, "A certain number of birds are always going to die during migrations."

At an attractive and informative rest stop provided by an oil company, I walked a short path through the woods. Signs describe how the "ultimate plan" is to return the land to its original state once the oil is extracted. There is no mention of the fact that these forests and their inhabitants have taken many hundreds of years to establish favourable ecological environments. How is it possible that a pristine boreal forest can be returned to its original state even in several lifetimes? When will the moose, the deer, and the bear return to these areas? Who will live here when the oil is gone? These questions are left unanswered by the ultimate plan.

I came to Fort McMurray with an open mind, but based on my observations, I was forced to conclude that the oil industry is making a huge mess up here. The pollution generated by these Projects is one reason Canada comes in dead last among G-8 Countries regarding environmental stewardship. Again, the crux of the problem has to do with the rapacious energy demands of end users. Oil companies are simply attempting to meet consumer's ceaseless demand, while Federal and Provincial governments are delighted to be receiving billions of dollars of tax revenue from sales of petroleum products.

A billboard in town advertising for foster parents stated: "Nobody can do everything, but everybody can do something." This slogan seems applicable to end users of petroleum products: Everybody can do something to reduce his or her energy needs. Also, there must be some middle ground between those who support a "full-steam ahead" approach to exploiting this unsustainable resource and radical environmentalists who oppose any further development. I heard on the news that Greenpeace had a "sit-in" at one of the Projects a few weeks after my visit. Presumably, this action was intended to make a statement to both the United States' President Obama and Canada's Prime Minister Harper who were meeting in Washington to discuss energy, among other matters. The protesters left after a few days with assurances they would not be charged for trespassing, but no assurances that anything would change. Nothing changed, but at least they did something.

Prior to leaving the next day, I visited the Oil Sands Discovery Centre where various interactive exhibits are provided to educate the public about open-pit mining, steam-assisted extraction, the tailing ponds, upgrading the bitumen, pipelining across North America, and environmental stewardship. It was here I learned about the size of the machinery, the elephant analogy, and the intention to make even bigger shovels and trucks. I suspect the "Largest Truck in the World" at Sparwood, BC would fit easily into the back of one of these monsters. The last sentence in their brochure sums it up nicely: "Protecting the environment is a shared responsibility involving industry, government, and consumers of hydrocarbon products." The question remains, what must each of these participants do to reach a sane middle ground?

After visiting the oil sands, I read Andrew Nikiforuk's *Tar Sands*, which compellingly condemns the ecological carnage occurring in Alberta. To his credit, he provides "Twelve Steps to Energy Sanity" including

- imposing a two-million-barrels-a-day cap that would give the governments of Alberta and Canada time to test and regulate cleaner technologies;
- eliminating toxic tailings ponds;
- creating a long-term plan; and
- establishing real-time reclamation programs.

Nikiforuk also provides practical advice for individual consumers like you and me: Power down. Eat local food. Walk more. Travel less.

I was okay until the last one. Following his advice would make this the end of our travels across Canada!

Back in Edmonton, we continued to be lambasted by severe weather, especially in the afternoons. Next to southern Ontario's "Tornado Alley," Alberta is reported to have the second largest number of tornadoes in Canada. We were surprised at the ferocity of the weather, apparently caused by warm air from the Pacific colliding with cold air from the Polar Regions.

On several occasions, we battened down the hatches and waited until the lightening and thunder abated, which couldn't come soon enough for Elly: *I was not impressed, pacing frantically, hiding under the table, waiting for a sane equilibrium to return.*

I once tried an experiment to see if I could reduce Elly's fear of thunder using Systematic Desensitization, a therapy commonly employed with humans who exhibit irrational fears (phobias). First, I obtained a recording of a thunderstorm from the local library; then played it softly while giving Elly treats. The theory is that a patient cannot be relaxed and anxious at the same time. So, if I kept my little patient relaxed, with treats, and gradually increased the volume of the noxious event, she should not show signs of anxiety. And she didn't. Over several days, no matter how loud I played the recording, she showed no reaction. Was she cured? I thought so. But no... during the very next thunderstorm, she was just as anxious as ever.

After speaking with a marine biologist who records and plays back whale sounds, I learned that she got the same non-reaction from whales using standard recording devices. Only when she used a sophisticated and expensive recording machine, did the whales respond to the play back. Apparently, the full range of frequencies encompassed in thunder, while perceptible to the canine ear, is not perceptible to the human ear and therefore not recorded on standard machines. I thus ended my experiment, but continue to wonder whether proper instrumentation might have reduced Elly's fear of thunder, a fear quite common in the canine world. As is so often mentioned at the conclusion of a psychological study... more research is needed.

In her bon-voyage card, Jo wrote, "Enjoy your onward journey into the sunrise." To be truthful, although we headed east for most of our trip, we never once drove into the sunrise. Leisurely mornings meant we usually got underway by noon or later. Just east of Edmonton at Vegreville, we pulled into a parking lot to view the world's largest Easter egg, nearly 8 metres long. This brightly coloured aluminum egg, which Ukrainians call a "Pysanka," was constructed to commemorate the early Ukrainian settlements in this area. An ethnic restaurant serving perogies and cabbage rolls would likely do well at this site, but no one was there to register comments, so we left.

3

SASKATCHEWAN

"Between the blush at dawn and dusk the long kiss of land and sky, bare against each other."

From "The Prairie" in This Land by Ken Odland

The sun shown brightly as we crossed the border into the neighbouring province of Saskatchewan. Temperatures approached 30° Celsius, about 10 degrees above normal for September. Immediate impressions, as seen from the highway, were checkerboard fields of amber, ochre, and green.

Fall is harvest time in the prairies and many farmers were taking advantage of the fine weather to collect their crops. On distant horizons, columns of dust rose behind tractors pulling reaping machines. Grain elevators, always beside railroad tracks, were prominent landmarks in most small towns.

British Columbia's landscape is mostly mountainous; Alberta has mountains to the west and prairie to the east; Saskatchewan, at least the southern section, is endless flat prairie. Two tongue-in-cheek sayings that capture the essence of this flatness: If your dog runs away from home, you can watch it for days; Saskatchewanians when visiting British Columbia complain that the mountains block their view! A scenic drive through southern Saskatchewan doesn't exist unless you have a particular attraction to grain fields, combines, and cows.

I love this route Dad ... just keep driving!

Elly and Buster, admiring the prairies in Saskatchewan

After a five-hour drive, one of the longest of our trip, we arrived at a Saskatoon soccer arena, site of a weekend Fly Ball tournament. Sandy's friend from Edmonton had several dogs in competition. Since the trailer was conveniently located in the parking lot, Linda used our pullout cot for an evening, rather than sleep in her already crowded van with the dogs.

Fly Ball involves two teams of dogs, four to a team, competing against each other. Two 51-foot lanes are set up with four hurdles spaced every ten feet. The first two dogs are released simultaneously by their handlers, run and jump the hurdles, retrieve a ball by pressing on a tread peddle, and return to their handlers. Then the second two dogs are released and so on until all four dogs have run. The team with the lowest combined time wins.

Handlers strive to minimize the time between the returning dog and the released dog passing the finish/start line. Judges sit at the line to ensure the returning dog's nose is across before the released dog's nose reaches the line. Anticipated releases are critical to keeping team times low.

Dogs barked enthusiastically, obviously keen to race. Elly, as a spectator, occasionally barked right along with them. I asked her, "What are you barking at?"

I'm not sure, but isn't this exciting? Arf, Arf, Arf!

She can be such a pack animal at times. Fly Ball is not a sport at which Elly would excel, given her tentative approach to negotiating the four steps on our trailer. It takes several abortive tries before she finally commits to going up or down, which is understandable, having fallen a few times over the years. *Consider me cautious and careful, not dangerous and dareful.*

A kindred spirit of Elly's, also a poodle, pranced her way from start to finish in 20 seconds. In comparison, the fastest dogs covered the distance in 15 seconds; one dog, a golden retriever, ran in 13 seconds.

The owner boasted that his dog was "the fastest Fly Ball dog in Canada." He hoped to have a run-off one day to claim title to the fastest in the world. I suspect if this sport gains in popularity, random doping tests are sure to follow.

At the event, I asked a lady from Moose Jaw, Saskatchewan where that city was located. She quipped, "About six feet from the moose's ass."

After snickering, she said that it was in the direction we were headed, southeast and a great place to visit: "Take the Tunnel Tours, visit the Spa, and check out the largest moose in the world."

The name "Moose Jaw" derives from a Cree word "Moosegaw," meaning "Warm Breezes," aptly named but totally unrelated to the anatomical part of a moose.

At the Visitor Centre, Mac the Moose, a towering concrete and steel structure, dominates the landscape. Elly had never seen a moose, but I was surprised at her lack of reaction. *I never looked up so I only saw the legs and thought they were trees.*

The receptionist also suggested we visit the Spa and take the Tunnel Tours during our two-day stay at a nearby campground.

We spent an hour relaxing in the Spa's mineral-rich water while I tried to memorize the flags of every country in the world, suspended from the ceiling above the expansive pool. Fortunately, no recall exam was required to exit the facility.

Afterward, we took both Tunnel Tours under the downtown streets.

"Chicago Connection" was a light-hearted venture into the hide-a-way of the notorious gangster Al Capone, who reportedly came to Moose Jaw during Prohibition to lay low when Chicago lawmen put the heat on his illegal booze activities. Several theme-dressed actors provided interactive commentary while guiding our small group from one hidden room to another. The realistic banter of Al's gals and goons gave us a taste of his high and low-living existence.

"Passage to Fortune" was a heavy-hearted venture into the early history of Chinese immigrants who came to Canada at great personal expense to make a better life for themselves and their families. An actor guide led our group through the cramped, damp rooms of an underground laundry where a ruthless entrepreneur forced several hundred employees to live in deplorable conditions during the 1880's. It's yet another poignant example of the inhumane treatment of minorities in Canada, a precursor to the internment of Japanese Canadians and the placement of Native Canadians in residential schools. One can only hope that the telling of these stories in various formats will help prevent future abuse of human rights in Canada and throughout the world.

We waved goodbye to Mac the Moose and headed east on the twinned Trans-Canada Highway (#1). Amidst a discussion about the fine weather we were having, an almost imperceptible brown cloud appeared ahead and a muffled machine-gun sound occurred — dah, dah, dah, dah, dah, dah, dah, dah — within a span of seconds. It took me a few moments to figure out what had just happened. Caught beneath the windshield wipers were the bodies of several dead bees. Apparently, we had collided with a swarm of bees crossing the highway at exactly the wrong time. At first opportunity, I pulled over and found dozens of dead bees impaled on the grill and radiator. I looked for the revered queen bee among the victims. Not seeing her, I assumed the remaining swarm continued their journey to an indeterminate destination, much as we were doing.

Near the Saskatchewan-Manitoba border, we diverted south and dry camped at a Casino on an Indian Reserve. This type of camping refers to not being hooked up to services: water, electricity, or sewer. Our rig allowed dry camping for several days, provided we had provisioned with water and emptied our grey-water and black-water holding tanks beforehand. Typically, we would access a campground after a day or two of dry camping to replenish water and dump our tanks.

Our diversion was also intended to check out the world's largest North-West Mounted Police statue at Redvers, Saskatchewan. This horse-and-rider statue towered above us and scared the dickens out of Elly. *That is one big horse—definitely not a hay bale!*

At first, she kept her distance but after some gentle coaxing, approached to a position underneath where she looked straight up, probably half expecting the big fellow to start moving. Of course, he didn't, and within minutes, she relaxed enough to frolic on the grass.

Elly at NWMP statue in Redvers, Saskatchewan

The North-West Mounted Police (NWMP) was established in 1873 to provide a police function in the Northwest Territories, a large section of Canada above the three western provinces. Over the ensuing 50 years, their jurisdiction expanded to include most of Canada. In 1920, their name was changed to the Royal Canadian Mounted Police. Today, the RCMP, commonly called "Mounties," in cooperation with provincial and municipal police forces, offer a wide range of police functions throughout Canada. Their red-serge ceremonial uniforms are as Canadian as the Maple Leaf and their stoic professionalism is respected worldwide.

Our rig parked in a farmer's field in Saskatchewan

Our curiosity about the varieties of roadside crops prompted me to pull onto a farmer's property. We were soon discussing crop rotation with the farmer who asked if we would like to ride in the combine while his son, a high-school senior, harvested canola. We jumped at the opportunity! For the next hour, we relished in the sights and smells of rural Canada, learning how the combine separates canola seeds from stalks and how the seeds are augered into a truck for transfer to temporary storage tanks. Later, they would be hauled to a grain elevator, which would in turn deposit them into railroad cars bound for processing plants or seaports for shipment abroad.

The whole family contributed in various ways; The son drove the combine, his mother drove the truck, and his younger sister made the meals. We were impressed with how hard farmers work. In good weather, they often sow (plant), swath (cut down), or combine (pick up) crops 21 hours a day, sometimes helping their neighbours as well. The father explained that the winter chores of repairing and maintaining machinery can be even more work intensive than planting and harvesting.

Because of this year's fine summer weather, grain yields were higher than normal in southern Saskatchewan. Our Visitor's Guide reported that

Canada leads the world in the export of lentils, peas, and chickpeas with Saskatchewan accounting for the majority of that production. The father told us these "pulse crops" put nitrogen back into the soil, thereby reducing the need for fertilizer when planting canola, wheat, or barley the following year. We were fortunate meeting such hospitable people to provide a glimpse of farm life in southern Saskatchewan. My respect for farmers, their knowledge, skills, and work ethic, increased enormously because of this chance encounter.

Elly also had an exciting couple of hours in the truck, watching several barnyard cats wandering about. *I like it here. Maybe someday, we can buy a farm?*

"We'll see," I replied. Actually, it does have a nice ring to it: Old Mac-Donald had a farm....

Crossing the border into Manitoba, I noted a sign THE FRIENDLY PROVINCE, which nicely described each of the three provinces we had already visited. Friendliness seemed to be a common denominator among Canadians wherever we went.

Larry MacDonald, Ph.D.

4

MANITOBA

"Freeing the Spirit, Fulfilling Potential Together"

Sign on wall at St. Amant Centre, Winnipeg

For some inexplicable reason, route numbers change at provincial borders. Route 13 in Saskatchewan changed to Route 2 at the Manitoba border. Go figure! As we drove eastward, we noticed oil pumps scattered across the fields, moving slowly up and down like giant grasshoppers eating. Farmers receive royalties from oil companies when they operate pumps on farm property. Our farmer friend lamented, "I've never been fortunate enough to have oil on any of my farms, even though I could throw rocks at the pumps on my neighbour's land. I guess I was meant to work for a living."

We also saw, for the first time, expansive fields of golden sunflowers ripe for harvest. This region, the Sunflower Belt, has ideal soil and weather conditions, allowing Manitoba to produce over 85% of the sunflower crops in Canada.

Finally, we noticed an increasing number of yellow brick homes similar to those in Ontario, the neighbouring province to the east. Most of the brick homes further west had been red in colour. Accustomed to red brick, I found the yellow brick homes to be statelier looking. Could the opposite be true? Would locals familiar with yellow brick find red brick homes to be statelier? Elly answered my question: *The color of brick doesn't determine the stateliness of a home. The design does. Build two doghouses out of different color brick ... the statelier one will be larger with a chimney and front porch.* An Ontario man we met later told us yellow brick houses were favoured by German settlers, whereas Scots and Irish preferred red.

We camped in the small town of Souris, famous for its suspended foot bridge over the Souris River. A plaque mentions that anyone who crosses the bridge becomes a citizen of Souris, so we took Elly across.

She was a little perplexed with the swaying movement but persevered with encouragement. *I did it both ways, with Mom and Dad's help!*

We didn't have the heart to tell her that she was now eligible to pay municipal taxes.

Elly and Sandy on suspension bridge in Souris, Manitoba

Peacocks in a nearby bird reserve strutted about, occasionally spreading their tails in a magnificent show of colour. A sign indicated that only males are called "peacocks" while females are called "peahens." Who knew? I added it to my Trivia File.

We continued on to Brandon, the province's second largest city with a population of 43,000. After camping overnight at a shopping centre, we drove a short distance eastward to the town of Portage La Prairie. Passing by the Assiniboine River, we noticed smatterings of white on green grass, resembling the vestiges of an early autumn snowfall. On closer inspection, what looked like snow was actually down feathers from thousands of geese that were flocking along the river's edge, eating grass in preparation for their annual southerly migration. Although some people refer to these birds as "Canadian" geese, they are properly known as Canada geese, even when they live in the US...more bird trivia.

Our intention was to visit the Indian Residential School Museum, advertised on the website of the Manitoba Historical Society. We had some difficulty locating this facility, as there was no sign in front of the building. In fact, there was no museum; just a two-story brick building that had served as a residential school from 1916 to 1975. Upon entering, we were greeted by a native woman employed by Long Plain First Nations to manage their on-site adult Employment and Training Program. She willingly offered a tour, showing us the dorms, classrooms, and a few remaining artifacts, including a cot, sinks, and toilets. Elly was allowed to accompany us to the delight of several students we encountered.

Our tour guide had attended several other residential schools and, when prompted by questions, willingly shared her personal experiences with us. She spoke about the harsh treatment, limited access to family, and the poor quality of food. On one occasion, her ill sister had thrown up in her porridge bowl and was forced to eat her own vomit. For some minor infraction, this same girl, branded "Devil Child," was kept in a room and badly beaten for three days, then forced to stand on a table in the cafeteria, displaying her welts and bruises before other students to keep them in line. The tour guide confided that she herself "walked on eggshells for fear of offending the nuns and priests." On the positive side, she commented that residential schools did provide her with an education, which she wouldn't have received on the reserve, allowing her to eventually earn a Master's Degree.

Having visited the Holocaust Museum in Israel and the Anne Frank Museum in Amsterdam, the tour guide said, "We have to tell our story in the building in which it happened." Unfortunately, an Aboriginal committee that had applied for a government grant to convert the school into a museum was denied funding. Perhaps the government didn't want to support a project that reflects badly on a previous administration? We left, hopeful that other financial resources would allow this project to proceed, thus preserving an important but tragic chapter in Native Canadian history.

Later, I was able to obtain a report released in 1994 by the Assembly of First Nations, *Breaking the Silence...An Interpretive Study of Residential School Impact and Healing as Illustrated by the Stories of First Nations Individuals.* These stories document the long-term consequences of residential schools: the loss of cultural identity, loss of language, loss of self-determination, loss of self respect, and loss of community left many Aboriginals unable to fit into either native or white society, leading to excessive use of alcohol and drugs to ease the anguish. As noted in the Executive Summary:

"The harsh and damaging environment experienced by many adult survivors of the residential school system has resulted in the carry-over of maltreatment into present day situations which are now affecting today's First Nation youth. The intergenerational cycle of patterns of abuse and mistrust stemming from years of residential schooling has had widespread impact on First Nations people everywhere and is a contributing factor in the breakdown of the family, the community and the cultural fabric of Aboriginal peoples in Canada."

A short distance away in Portage La Prairie, we took a driving tour of the Manitoba Development Centre, a residential and day-program facility for adults with developmental disabilities. In Alberta and British Columbia over the past several decades, "Normalization" has been the guiding principle, promoting the belief that segregating people with disabilities was not only stigmatizing, but also detrimental to personal growth. Community Behavioural Services, the program I directed in Alberta, helped hundreds of individuals return from institutions such as this one to independent living. Application of the principle required resources and government commitment, but proved to be very successful. Unfortunately, we arrived after business hours so were unable to talk to anyone about their programs and plans for the future. As we drove out the front gate of this segregated facility, I felt like I had stepped back in time 20 years.

We continued on to Winnipeg, the capital city of over 600,000, about half the population of Manitoba. Before getting underway each day, Sandy would program our GPS to locate intended destinations. This little gizmo, attached to a beanbag on our dashboard, was invaluable, helping us navigate city streets or find campsites, gas stations, restaurants, and even a veterinarian on one occasion.

"Andy" (a favourite uncle who was an inveterate back-seat driver) kept us from getting lost more than once with his constant reminders of where and when to turn. If we missed the turn, he would "recalculate" the next shortest distance to our destination. As we traversed a ring road on the outskirts of Winnipeg, Andy began vibrating across the dashboard and Buster complained in his usual manner about the bumpy ride.

When we mentioned the rough roads to a local man, he quipped, "It's not called 'Winterpeg' for nothing." Severe winters cause buckling of the roadways, the worse we encountered up to this point. Unbeknownst to us, even rougher roads lay ahead.

While camping for a night in the parking lot of a downtown casino, we learned about the contribution of Manitoba Lottery Corporations to Manitobans. Pamphlets in the casino indicated that during the past year, nearly $300 million was allocated to non-profit community projects and government programs including health care, education, social services, and economic development. Gambling is big business in Manitoba, as it is in most provinces, so I was pleased to learn that free educational and counseling services were available to those affected by gambling addiction. As we walked through the casino, I was astounded and saddened by the many pasty-faced seniors playing slot machines, some two at a time, with cigarettes dangling from their lips. While many consider it a form of entertainment, I would rather have a root canal. I'm more inclined to play Blackjack, which requires at least some decision-making. Win or lose, it's always quicker than playing the slots so I get to inhale less second-hand smoke!

Since Winnipeg has much to offer tourists, we relocated to a nearby campground for a few days of exploration. Our first stop was St. Amant Centre, another facility providing services to people with disabilities. Several staff that I had hired in Alberta received their practicum training here in conjunction with their courses at the University of Winnipeg. Our timing was excellent as the Volunteer Coordinator greeted us at the door and kindly offered us a tour. Their services are more akin to what we provided in Alberta, an Outreach Service in homes, schools, and vocational settings. As well, individuals admitted to specialized residential facilities were expected to return home, to foster care, or to small group homes. I was impressed with St. Amant's focus on self-determination and integrated social activities for the nearly 1000 individuals served each year.

Winnipeg is home to the Royal Canadian Mint where our coins are made, over one billion each year. Its impressive entrance displays flags of every country lining both sides of the curved boulevard. Unfortunately, our timing was off. The next tour was not scheduled for another hour so we decided to skip it and instead, visit the Riel House National Historic Site where Louis Riel, the famous Métis leader and founder of Manitoba, grew up in the mid 1800's.

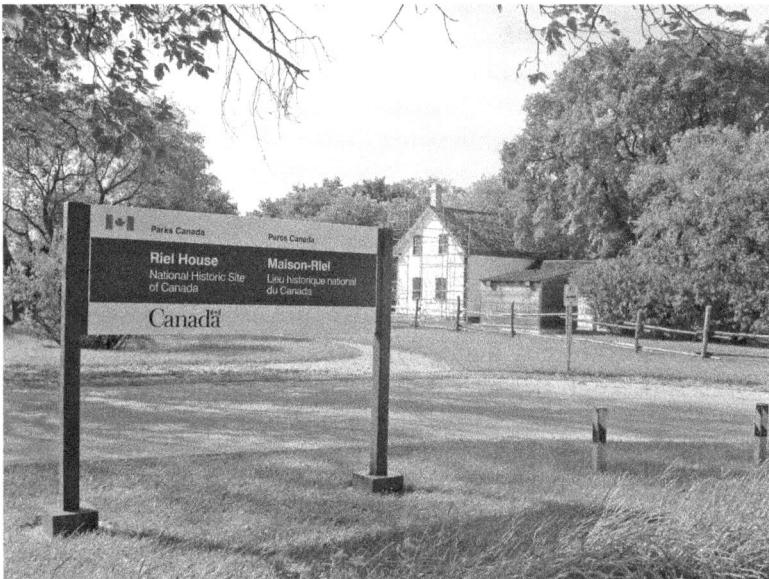

Louis Riel's childhood home, under renovation, in Winnipeg, Manitoba

Although we were too late in the season for a tour of the small wooden bungalow, the custodian prompted us to pick ripened vegetables in the garden, which we later shared with Sandy's aunt and uncle in Ontario. He suggested we visit St. Boniface, the largest French-Canadian community west of Quebec, where we would find the gravesite of Louis Riel in the cemetery of St. Boniface Cathedral, 190 avenue de la Cathedrale. In this community, street signs are in French and everyone has strong accents, providing a multicultural atmosphere in shops and restaurants. Sandy practiced her French to the delight of several bilingual waiters and shopkeepers.

In the Old Market Square of The Forks district, a fellow tourist mentioned that Winnipeg was considered "The Murder Capital of Canada." I did some on-line research and discovered that Richmond, a city near Vancouver, recently took over that dubious honour. In both cities, the majority of residents were unaffected since most homicides were drug and gang related. Nonetheless, travelers everywhere need to be aware of their immediate surroundings, especially in large cities where desperate people gravitate.

Elly remained in the trailer during our daily excursions, but her ears perked up when we recounted our ventures in "The French Quarter." *Did you happen to see any poodles, you know, males?* At ten years of age (which is what, about 70 in human years?) she is still feisty.

"No," I answered, "but we did see a couple of winnipugs."

Oh Dad, you're such a kidder!

An hour's drive southeast of Winnipeg is the small city of Steinbach, which I assumed was a cartographer's misprint and should have been "Steinbeck." But no, a receptionist at the Travel Centre said it's a German derivative meaning, "Stony Brook." We meandered through their Mennonite Heritage Village: over twenty historical buildings built in the late 1800's provided an absorbing look at the Mennonite pioneer experience.

Established in the 1500's, this religious sect began arriving in Canada in the mid 1700's typically settling into a simple, rural lifestyle. Today, over 200,000 Mennonites reside in Canada, mostly in Ontario and the western provinces, where farming supports their self-sufficient communities. Downtown, a local gentleman told us Steinbach was once called the "City of Automobiles" because of the large number of auto dealerships. Along the main boulevard, a sizable number were still operating.

Returning north to Highway #1 and continuing east, the landscape changed gradually but distinctly from prairie to scrub brush and forests as we approached the Ontario border.

We passed several fruit and vegetable stands—not intentionally, but the lack of advanced signage did not allow us to slow down sufficiently to pull in. Surely, I mused, the last stand before the Ontario border would have a LAST CHANCE sign. It did not. We crossed devoid of fresh produce, other than the squash and tomatoes we had picked at the Riel homestead.

Sandy said that if I had my way, "there would be signs all over the world."

"Of course," I concurred, "including at least one in Manitoba which would have benefited us as well as the vendor selling fruits and vegetables."

Larry MacDonald, Ph.D.

5

ONTARIO

"Dreams are made if people only try. I believe in miracles...I have to...because somewhere the hurting must stop."

**Quote from the late Terrance Stanley Fox
at Terry Fox Memorial, Thunder Bay, Ontario, 1981**

As we crossed the border, the Trans-Canada Highway changed from Highway #1 to Route #17. Mapmakers also saw fit to divide the Trans-Canada in Ontario, requiring several different route numbers, each designated by a small maple leaf logo. Looking at a map of Canada, I was further perplexed by the fact that Quebec and Nova Scotia use route numbers other than #1 for the Trans-Canada even though it is their major undivided highway. Logic returned in Newfoundland where #1 was appropriately inserted within the maple leaf logo.

At the border, the road surface changed from bumpy concrete to smooth blacktop, presumably reflecting Ontario's greater prosperity relative to Manitoba. On both sides of the highway, rock outcroppings began to appear where road-construction crews had blasted away the mostly rock substrata that forms much of northern Ontario. This Canadian Shield consists of volcanic rock formed hundreds of millions of years ago, stretching north from the United States through the Great Lakes region to the Arctic Ocean. As we continued on to Kenora, we noted an increasing amount of graffiti on the rock faces. One was inscribed in large painted letters: #1 DAD, YOUR GIRLS, a tribute that most likely, would have made papa proud! Much of the older graffiti had been crudely covered by patches of pink and red paint rolled onto brown and grey rock surfaces, giving the appearance of a sixth-grade painting project gone amuck.

I once developed a business plan, intended to provide some extra income after retirement. My objective was to remove graffiti from rocks and bridge abutments by spraying over it with a colour that matched the surface colour. Paints, spray guns, and related equipment would be transported in a sizable motorhome, allowing me to work south to Arizona in the winter and back north to British Columbia in the summer, another objective. Income would derive from fee-for-service contracts with various agencies such as Parks Canada or municipal, state, and federal governments responsible for the desecrated sections of land. I even chose a clever name for this business, RAGS—Remove All Graffiti Services (I was thinking Rags to Riches). But, like so many of my brilliant ideas, nothing came of it.

We had planned to dry-camp at a Kenora shopping centre, but a plethora of signs indicated that RV overnight parking was prohibited by city ordinance. Obviously, I don't detest signs, but I do sometimes get annoyed at the bureaucrats that authorize such signs!

When I asked a store manager whether RV's park here overnight, he said they sometimes do, but he couldn't authorize us to do so and we might be asked to move in the middle of the night. To avoid the hassle, we parked instead beside a nearby baseball diamond where a co-ed softball game was in progress. The women's head scarves and plain long dresses identified them as a group of Mennonites enjoying the balmy weather.

The next morning, we drove through downtown Kenora, which features "Huskie the Muskie," a 13-metre-high fish sculpture promoting the excellent recreational fishing available in northern Ontario. Continuing east for several hours, we arrived at a campground near Ignace. Along the way, we noted some very informative and effective signs for speeding on Highway 17. When the speed limit was 90 kph, the signs showed the increasing fines for speeds above the limit: $95 for 110 kph, $220 for 120 kph, and higher fines for higher speeds. They certainly grabbed my attention. Perhaps such signs should be erected on Alberta's Highway of Death to slow down speeders? We also passed a sign LARGE VEHICLES NEED MORE ROOM, advice desperately needed in Vancouver.

The next morning, we struck up a conversation with two Japanese lads who had pitched a tent nearby. Their overburdened road bikes indicated they were roughing it, so we invited them in for breakfast.

They readily accepted, and over the next hour, we learned that Daiki and Nari were biking from Banff, Alberta, where they had worked for the summer, to Toronto, Ontario.

It was Daiki's birthday, so we stuck a candle in a piece of coffee cake and sang "Happy Birthday." Elly howled along in her own unique way, much to their delight. *I also sing along to accordion and bagpipe music, in spite of not having any musical training. I guess I'm just musically inclined!*

We packed their lunch and shouted "Sayonara" as they rode out of the campground. An hour later, we passed them with a fanfare of horn blowing and waving. They were averaging 300 km a day on their bikes. In comparison, we were averaging just 50 km a day since leaving Powell River two and a half months ago, rarely driving more than 400 kilometres at a stretch—they would reach Toronto long before us.

When I folded our map of Canada in half, the crease ran through Ignace, the halfway point of our journey. The breadth of Ontario surprised me, wider than the three western provinces of Manitoba, Saskatchewan, and Alberta combined. Over one-third of Canada's entire population of 33 million lives in the province of Ontario.

That evening, we camped in the parking lot of a major retail store in Thunder Bay, a busy seaport on the northern shore of Lake Superior. This lake is the largest in the world, containing ten percent the world's fresh water, more water than all the other four Great Lakes combined, plus three extra Lake Erie's.

Canada has more lakes than any other country in the world—over 3 million. Nearly 10% of Canada's land mass is composed of fresh water, which will become an even more valuable commodity as the world's supply diminishes. Within a few generations, I suspect wars will be fought over water rather than ideology, religion, or oil.

One of the strangest signs we saw on our trip was on a city street in Thunder Bay: NO PARKING, 2-HOUR MAXIMUM. I asked a local gentleman what the sign meant; he replied, "Darned if I know."

If there is such a thing as reincarnation, I want to come back as a Signage Engineer, whose responsibility it would be to evaluate the need for and appropriateness of signs. A large dollop of common sense would be the only requirement.

We followed the shoreline of Lake Superior for the next couple of days, stopping at several overlooks that showcase the majesty of this region. Just east of Thunder Bay is a monument in honour of Terry Fox, another Canadian icon.

Terry's effort to run across Canada on one leg to raise money for cancer inspired and united a nation. After dipping his artificial leg in the Atlantic Ocean on April 12, 1980, this courageous young man ran a marathon (42 kilometres) a day, every day, for a distance of 5,373 kilometres. Unfortunately, on September 1, his cancer had spread to his lungs, forcing him to abandon his Marathon of Hope just east of this site.

Terry Fox memorial near Thunder Bay, Ontario

Although Terry died less than a year later, his dream to increase awareness and find a cure for cancer in his self-proclaimed "world of miracles" lives on in the hearts and minds of Canadians. In 1999, nearly 20 years after his feat, Terry Fox was named Canada's Greatest Hero in a national survey. To date, mostly through annual runs, more than $500 million has been raised worldwide for cancer research—a Canadian hero, indeed.

While driving along "Terry Fox Courage Highway" east of Thunder Bay, Sandy commented that the undulating ribbon of two-lane highway bordered by rock outcroppings and bush, brought back childhood memories of her family taking summer holidays in northern Ontario. Puffy white clouds were forming in the blue sky.

Sandy's mom used to say, "On a cloudy day, there's no reason to be bored." She would often look up and find familiar shapes, usually animals, and point them out to Sandy, who carries on the tradition: "Look over there—a lobster."

Hereabouts, locals refer to the forests as "bush." Scatterings of tamarack, elm, and birch, bathed in brilliant sunlight, were just beginning to turn shades of yellow, orange, and red. Along the highway, occasional small towns, replete with signage for bait and boat shops, serve as supply bases for recreational activities such as fishing, hunting, and paddling.

Again, on the subject of signage, Highway 17 provides TURNOUTS— short stretches of pavement intended for slower vehicles to pull over to let traffic pass. Unfortunately, more often than not we would drive right by these turnouts, unable to stop in time because of our greater stopping distance than a car. This discourteous action was likely upsetting the drivers lined up behind us, but we had no choice in the matter. What logic prevails to erect Passing-Zone signs 10 kilometres in advance of a passing zone while Turnout signs are erected at the entrance to a turnout?

A cook at our campground restaurant near Marathon informed us that gold mining had become the primary source of employment since the value of gold went up and the forestry industry shut down. "It was not pretty," he said, "long-time forestry workers were laid off without severance or pensions. Some found employment in the gold mines but many are still unemployed, disgruntled, and contemplating lawsuits."

We drove away amidst a dissonance of natural beauty and human misfortunes, with hope that justice will prevail in the upcoming court cases.

The huge statue of a Canada goose, with outstretched wings, greeted us as we pulled into the Tourist Information Centre in Wawa, an Ojibway name for "Wild Goose." Their brochure refers to the statue as the largest of its kind in Canada and one of the most photographed landmarks in North America. (Did you ever wonder who keeps track of such statistics?).

Author at Goose Statue in Wawa, Ontario

This 8.5-metre steel structure was erected in 1960 to commemorate the last link of the Trans-Canada highway. Because of its size, we're not sure Elly even recognized it as a bird since she showed no reaction as we walked toward it. *I did see the famous bird but my prior training of "just watch, don't chase" served me well. Anyway, I'm not sure what I would have done if I had chased and caught that big quacker.*

During our photo shoot, we felt the first raindrops since leaving Edmonton two weeks earlier. The rain continued almost daily for the next few weeks, reminiscent of damp, dreary winters on the West Coast.

After overnighting on a street beside scenic Lake Wawa, we left the Trans-Canada and headed east onto Highway 101. An interesting phenomenon occurred along this less-traveled section of two-lane road. Several drivers of recreational vehicles waved at us as we passed, something that never happened on the Trans-Canada.

In psychology, this behaviour is related to the well-researched "by-stander effect," whereby the chances of a person in need of assistance and actually receiving it decreases as the number of people present increases. Take a man with a disabled vehicle...he is less likely to receive help on a freeway than on a country road. Presumably, multiple "bystanders" on the freeway conjointly share responsibility for providing assistance, which reduces each individual's responsibility. On a less traveled road, other drivers feel greater responsibility than they would on a freeway, prompting them to wave.

We decided to wave at every driver of a recreational vehicle along this road; most waved back. Of course, we would still have to compare these results with what we would obtain on a freeway to determine whether our bystander hypothesis is valid. Since we were on holidays, I suggested to Sandy that some other research-minded traveler could finish this study. As a rule, we found most RVers to be friendly: in campgrounds, they wave and chat readily like long-lost friends.

Shania Twain, the renowned country music singer, was born and raised in the small town of Timmins. After a night camping at a local retail store, we visited the Shania Twain Centre, featuring video simulations of her live concerts, a backstage experience, and memorabilia, all very popular with country music fans.

Not far away was a very busy Tim Horton's where we picked up coffees for the road. Beginning in Hamilton, Ontario in 1964, "Timmies" now has over 3000 coffee shops throughout Canada, making it another understated Canadian icon: coffee on a par with beavers and geese.

Along Highway #11 heading south, we passed the site of the recently held Temiskaming International Plowing Match, which seemed to be the topic of conversation with every person we met in Northern Ontario. Over 80,000 people attended this five-day plowing match, the largest community event ever held in these parts. It showcased all aspects of Ontario's agricultural, forestry, and mining industries along with competitive plowing, music, parades, and concerts.

Sandy's Uncle Stewart, whom she hadn't seen in ten years, invited us to visit him in New Liskeard. Fortunately, his driveway was just large enough for the trailer. He and his wife Eva were very accommodating during our five-day stay. A lot of "chin wagging" occurred around the kitchen table during meals and our nightly Bid Euchre games. Sandy's Aunt Laura and Uncle Walter also lived nearby so we got to catch up on their lives as well.

Stewart drove us around rural areas, pointing out some of the preparations for the plowing match. We especially liked the numerous individually dressed scarecrows adorning downtown streets, some swinging in the breeze from streetlights like high-flying trapeze acts. Also, large wooden quilt blocks hanging on barns, buildings, and businesses were used as signposts to guide tourists using a regional map.

On another day, we visited Cobalt, a mining town between 1903 and 2003. This was a fascinating trip back in time for Stewart as he and his brother Lloyd had both worked in the mines.

Numerous mining artifacts were on display. Stewart explained how they worked and how dangerous, noisy, and dusty it was in the mineshafts. In those days, no one wore ear or lung protection devices, which likely contributed to a severe loss of hearing for Stewart and fatal emphysema for his late brother.

Many miners never survived to retirement. Stewart was fortunate and got out in the nick of time—on his very last day of work after five years in the mine, he narrowly escaped being crushed by a falling boulder.

On yet another day in the morning, we visited a nearby sheep ranch where the wool was washed, spun into fibres, and then woven into fabrics, duplicating a process carried out over 100 years ago.

In the afternoon, Eva showed us her dairy farm, now operated by her adult son and grandson. They demonstrated how a robotic feeder on an overhead track provided food for each cow as they stood in stalls waiting to be milked by machine. A computer chip attached to each cow's ear "told" the robot the appropriate blend and amount of feed it should dispense for best milk production.

Eva commented that dairy farming had come a long way since her days: feeding all cows the same diet and milking by hand. A framed plaque hung in her son's office DOING WHAT YOU LIKE IS FREEDOM; LIKING WHAT YOU DO IS HAPPINESS. I asked him if he was looking forward to retirement.

He replied, "Not really. I'm quite happy doin' what I'm doin'." He seemed as content as his computer-fed cows.

Fall colors in Northern Ontario

Leaving New Liskeard, we camped for a night in a parking lot in North Bay and contacted Sandy's aunt Viv, who drove us to a charming restaurant. There we all got reacquainted over dinner.

The next day, we stopped in at Orillia, hometown of Steven Leacock, a well-known author, and humorist during the early 1900's—Canada's counterpart to American born Samuel Clemens (Mark Twain). After nearly getting stuck on a narrow back street, we gave up searching for Leacock's home and continued on to Elmvale for a three-day visit with another of Sandy's relatives, her cousin Colin. He, with the help of his wife Suzie and their two adult sons, operate a dairy farm that had been passed down from his folks. Again, we came to appreciate the hard work and long hours that farmers put into making the various dairy products we purchase so easily from grocery shelves.

Elly kept a safe distance from the cows, especially those that stuck their heads through the pasture fence. *OK guys, or should I say gals, are you friend or foe? And how fast can you run?* Had we not coaxed her away, she would have spent the entire day ensnared in an approach-avoidance conflict.

She also had the same fascination with several cats that lived in the farmhouse. In the trailer, Elly was constantly vigilant at the window lest she miss their movements in the yard. We've noted a similar obsessive behaviour in campgrounds. If she sees a cat in a neighbour's rig, she'll spend an inordinate amount of time transfixed on the vehicle.

On our third day, Suzie invited us to attend a meeting of the Women's Institute, a charitable organization dedicated to improving the quality of life of its members, their families, and local communities. Established in 1919 in Ontario, hundreds of provincial branches meet monthly for personal growth and education of its members. Shortly before leaving for the meeting, Suzie received a phone call from the Chairperson telling her that the invited speaker, who had planned to talk about radical lifestyle changes, was unable to attend. Suzie asked whether we would be willing to "fill in" and talk about our recent lifestyle change. So we did, to the apparent delight of the dozen or so members in attendance.

During our presentation, one lady asked, "Do you feel guilty about always being on holidays."

I answered, "Not at all: we worked hard most of our lives and consider our extended holiday a well-deserved reward."

In retrospect, perhaps her question was whether we felt guilty because, from her perspective, we weren't contributing to a common good. Most in attendance were farmer's wives, typically conservative types, well-rooted with strong work ethics. Although I didn't take a poll, I suspect most either envied us or could not comprehend such a radical lifestyle change as we had made. In either case, if "Liking what you do is happiness," we were happy campers, and hoped the same for these ladies.

Three days of rain had the truck's tires spinning in the slick grass when we tried to depart. No worries. Colin hooked a chain from his tractor to our front end and pulled our rig effortlessly off the grass, through a muddy field, and onto a gravel roadway.

After a round of hugs, we headed west to Kincardine on the shore of Lake Heron where we stayed overnight in the parking lot of a bowling alley. Two more of Sandy's cousins live in this small town so we invited them and their husbands over for some vino and a long overdue chinwag.

The next morning, we drove a short distance south to Goderich, described on their welcome sign CANADA'S PRETTIEST TOWN. Situated on the eastern shore of Lake Huron, the town features a unique octagonal centre with trendy shops and restaurants, tree-lined streets, and overflowing flower baskets hanging from decorative lampposts. We dry camped for a couple of nights at a city park while visiting Pat, another of Sandy's cousins.

All totaled, Sandy has 22 cousins living in various towns in Ontario, and she planned to visit all of them. To make her job easier, Pat arranged for eight of the female cousins, within easy driving distance, to meet for dinner at a local restaurant.

While they were wining and dining, the guys all got together for beer and chicken wings at a local pub and talked fishing, hunting and football. Most were on a first-name basis with other patrons, so typical of small-town ambiance. One fellow described his work at the local Sifto Salt Mine, one of the world's largest salt companies. Every day, he takes an elevator 500 metres down and a rail car several kilometres under Lake Huron where he operates a shovel extracting rock salt. Large cargo ships transport the chunks of salt to various ports of call in the Great Lakes where it is further distributed throughout Canada and the United States. Sifto's finer salt is manufactured in an evaporator plant and packaged for table use.

The next day, Pat and her husband George escorted us around town showing us old mansions, new housing developments, the salt mine, and industries that manufacture yachts and bulldozers. After a casual lunch in the oldest historical building in Goderich, we said our farewells and headed 100 kilometres southeast to London. A local campground provided our base of operations while we visited friends and a few more of Sandy's cousins.

Elly was still responsive to the mention of Toby's name, cocking her head from side to side and looking around for her childhood sweetheart. We drove over to our friends' house and, sure enough, there was little Toby at the door, eagerly awaiting our arrival. Surprisingly, Elly only gave Toby a cursory sniff and then proceeded to search their house for the same two cats that had lived with Toby back in Edmonton. Puppy love is so fickle. *Don't get me wrong Toby, you're still my friend, but I have what my Dad calls a " feline fascination" whenever there is a cat around. So bug off...we can play later.*

Since Elly doesn't carry on this way with Buster, I wondered how long she would have to be exposed to these cats before the obsessive attraction wore off—certainly longer than the four hours of our visit, which was how long Elly kept watching these felines, wagging her tail and trailing after them whenever they moved from their perches on the couch and kitchen chairs.

We stayed at the campground for nearly a week until it closed October 15. Most campgrounds in Ontario close about that time because very few people camp when the weather gets colder. The day before we left, a blanket of snow covered the ground, lasting only a few hours. We moved the trailer to a friend's driveway for another week, since we couldn't cross the border just yet.

Canadians can only spend a maximum of six months a year in the United States, and we had already spent almost four months there on our trip to Arizona, returning April 26 to Canada. Instead of staying in the trailer, we were invited into a friend's house.

Anita, one of Sandy's co-workers when she worked in Ontario, is now officially retired, but boards dogs to earn extra income. Elly got lots of exercise interacting with them. Each morning, donning heavy sweaters, hats, and gloves, we would take them all for a walk through nearby woods where brown leaves blanketed the forest pathways.

Winter was indeed on the way. On October 27, 2009, we crossed the border—the longest land border in the world—at Port Huron, Ontario heading for Florida.

Six months later on April 24, we re-entered Canada at Thousand Islands, near Kingston, Ontario. Our original plan was to re-enter at New Brunswick, explore the eastern provinces, then work our way back to London in the fall. However, several seasoned travelers had advised us that springtime in the Maritimes was typically cool and most campgrounds would be closed. Southern Ontario, on the other hand, can be quite pleasant in April and May. Following the slogan on Ontario's license plate YOURS TO DISCOVER, we decided to continue our travels where we left off—in London.

Camping for several days near Kingston gave us an opportunity to visit two local attractions: Fort Henry, a 19th century military fortress, was built by the British on a prominent hillside overlooking Lake Ontario, the St. Lawrence River, and the Rideau Canal. Having never come under attack, the fortress was abandoned by the British Army in 1870. In 1938 after considerable restoration, it opened as a museum and has since been designated one of Canada's 167 National Historic Sites. Guided tours, exhibits, and educational programs were scheduled to begin later in the season. Standing on the ramparts provided a panoramic view of Kingston and the surrounding countryside. A security guard informed us that there were about 300 soldiers in the fortress when it was fully manned. "Today" he said, "there's just me."

Another National Historic Site, the Rideau Canal opened in 1832, connecting Kingston to Ottawa through a series of lakes, rivers, and locks. Each of 45 locks was designed to transport boats up or down from one water level to another. The original wooden lock at Kingston looked archaic with crude gears, levers, and gates but a local man assured us that it would be busy transporting recreational boats during the upcoming season.

Upon awakening on April 27, we were given a proper welcome back to Canada by snow flurries and a bone-chilling wind, reminding us why we went south for the winter. With stoic acceptance, we broke camp and proceeded onto Highway 401 on our way to London.

This highway, extending across the breadth of southern Ontario from Windsor to the Quebec border, is one of the widest and busiest roadways in North America. Approaching Toronto, it widens to nine lanes in one direction, insufficient to accommodate the heavy afternoon traffic, which slowed to a crawl at some interchanges. We were relieved to finally make it past Toronto and decided to spend the night in a campground near Milton, rather than risk arriving at London during rush hour.

A 150-kilometre section of "four-oh-one" between Trenton and Toronto was dedicated in 2007 as HIGHWAY OF HEROS, commemorating Canadian soldiers who died on foreign soil. Periodic signs displaying large red poppies remind motorists of the sacrifices that many have made to ensure others throughout the world can live in relative peace.

For the previous eight years, Canada's military had been engaged in Afghanistan, resulting in 142 fatalities at the date of our transit. Each of their bodies was flown to Trenton Air Force Base and then transported to the coroner's office in Toronto in a convoy of hearses and limousines carrying grieving families. Reportedly on these occasions, thousands of Canadians line overpasses, some standing solemnly, some saluting, and some waving flags to pay their respects.

Milton is a small town 40 kilometres west of Toronto that bills itself FASTEST GROWING COMMUNITY IN CANADA. Several new housing developments were nestled close to farmland and forests, far removed from the hustle and bustle of city life. Milton lies on the edge of the Niagara Escarpment, a prominent ridge of protected cliffs and forests running diagonally across southern Ontario. Its most famous feature is the cliff over which the Niagara River plunges to form Niagara Falls. Later, we would visit that natural wonder but we did cross the escarpment just west of Milton on our way to London.

With the trailer parked in a friend's driveway, Anita's home became our base of operations for the better part of a month, giving us ample time to re-visit friends and family. At the time of our visit, London was Canada's 10th largest city with a population of nearly a half million, serving as the central hub for surrounding communities. Its' nickname "Forest City" is due to the abundance of tree-lined streets, parks, and green areas. London, as reported annually in Maclean's Magazine, consistently ranks near the top of Canadian communities for quality of life, cultural activities, economic development, and a well-educated populace. The top-rated city has typically been Victoria, BC on Vancouver Island, which we did not visit during our cross-Canada trip.

London's weather in May was comfortable with a mix of sunshine and showers. Several severe thunderstorms occurred during our stay but fortunately no tornados. The city is located just below the infamous Tornado Alley, a narrow corridor extending from Windsor and Sarnia northeastward to Barrie. Cool breezes from Lake Huron and Lake Erie interact with hot unstable air streams from the Gulf of Mexico creating atmospheric conditions that spawn thunderstorms and tornadoes. The majority of damaging tornadoes that have occurred in Canada have been in Ontario.

Since Elly enjoyed playing with her friend Toby and with Anita's dogs, she would have been quite happy to stay in London. However, we just happen to be there on the May long weekend which includes Victoria Day, a public holiday intended to celebrate Queen Victoria's birthday and informally marking the beginning of the summer holiday season. Although Queen Victoria died in 1901, the holiday continues in celebration of the reigning Canadian monarch, currently Queen Elizabeth II.

Celebrations typically include organized fireworks displayed in outdoor venues. And since public ownership of fireworks is legal in Canada, backyard displays are commonplace. Elly panted and paced the whole weekend, until well after midnight. *What is it with people who get their kicks setting off firecrackers and scaring defenceless little puppies like me?*

I pointed out to her that these random pops, while annoying, were not harmful but it made no difference. She has always hated fireworks.

An applicable psychological principle known as Extinction maintains that repeated presentations of an aversive stimulus, such as a loud noise, with no consequences should eliminate a fearful reaction to that stimulus. Elly has heard thousands of firecrackers over the years, yet still displays her stereotypical reaction of panting, pacing, listening intently, and hiding behind chairs, sometimes even in the bathtub. I suspect the intermittent nature of these aversive events prevents her fearful behaviour from extinguishing. If I could expose her to fireworks every night for a month, she would most likely ignore them. *Try that little experiment with me Dad, and I'll ignore YOU!*

We had planned to leave London on Victoria Day but were delayed for a couple of weeks because of two unforeseen events. The first involved an incident of Buster biting Anita on the hand when she tried to pick him up by the scruff of his neck after he escaped into her back yard. The bite became infected, resulting in Anita being hospitalized for two days before being discharged with a bandaged hand. We agreed to stay until she felt capable of handling household chores on her own. Buster had never bitten anyone else, ever, so I guess it was his way of saying, "I dislike being picked up by the scruff of my neck."

The second involved five nursing kittens whose mother was killed by a car. Anita's friend Hedy took the kittens from a Rescue Centre into her home to nurture them. Sandy agreed to help. Every two hours, day and night, they syringe-fed and cuddled each one. Over a two-week period, the three weakest failed to thrive, two of them dying peacefully in Sandy's arms. The remaining two at five weeks of age were eating independently and playing joyfully together. Hedy planned to put them up for adoption in a few more weeks. Sandy had other ideas.

Interestingly, for the past year Anita had been feeding five feral cats that had taken up residence under a nearby trailer. On the same day that the third kitten died, three feral kittens that she hadn't seen before showed up for the evening meal. I wrote it off to coincidence. Anita being more spiritual interpreted it as a message from God: "I've taken three kittens into Heaven, so I'm giving you these three back to look after." In either case, they would be well looked after.

After Anita felt sufficiently recovered from her injury, we hitched up and doubled back on 401, diverting slightly south to Burlington for a visit with Sandy's childhood friend Barb and her husband Mike. With the trailer parked in their driveway, we would visit Toronto and Niagara Falls, two cities at opposite ends of the Golden Horseshoe, a densely populated region capping the western tip of Lake Ontario. I was impressed with Burlington's progressive recycling program, which reuses almost everything, including food scraps. They even provide a loose-leaf collection service in the fall. Residents, instead of bagging their leaves in plastic bags, simply rake them into the gutter for pick up by city street-sweepers.

Early on our second day, we all piled into Mike's van for an hour and a half drive on Queen Elizabeth Way, known as the QEW or the Queen E, to Toronto. We felt like kids on a field trip to the big city! Our first stop was the revolving restaurant of CN Tower, which provided lunch and a panoramic view of the city's buildings, harbour, airport, and freeways. Toronto, the capital of Ontario, is Canada's largest city at about five million, and appears to be growing rapidly. From our window seats, we counted over a dozen cranes building skyscrapers in the downtown area. Mike mentioned that the vertical structure supporting each crane becomes the elevator shaft after work is completed.

However logical that may sound, my subsequent research showed that the entire crane and supporting structure is actually removed by a series of smaller cranes, while the last crane is dismantled piece by piece. Occasionally, helicopters are used to lower the pieces. Elevator shafts are built separately.

The Tower also has an observation deck with sections of glass floor. Standing on the glass, one can look straight down 342 metres to the street below. Most visitors, us included, had to muster up courage to step onto the glass, even though it reportedly can hold the weight of a dozen elephants. In my younger days, I used to fly airplanes, hang glide, bungy jump, and sky dive, but I still get a tight ass whenever I approach the edge of a precipice, and this was no different. I visualized the headline: "Psychologist dies after falling through glass floor of CN Tower." Now wouldn't that spice up the story a bit?

After lunch, we took a small ferry around the harbour to view three natural islands that offer marinas, walking trails, a bird sanctuary, park, and the Billy Bishop Toronto City Airport. The airport was named in honour of a Canadian war hero who shot down more enemy planes than any other pilot during WWI. Since no cars are allowed on these islands, the airport is accessed from downtown by ferry, which according to our tour guide is the shortest in the world, taking just 37 seconds. Our ferry also provided an opportunity to photograph the skyline of Toronto, distinguished by the imposing CN tower which until recently was considered the tallest freestanding structure in the world. A skyscraper in Dubai has since captured that honour.

The remainder of our day was spent on a hop-on, hop-off tour bus, with a guide providing running commentary about twenty different Toronto neighbourhoods. We hopped off once to browse the "not to be missed" St. Lawrence Market, where merchants have been selling wares for over 200 years, making it Canada's oldest marketplace. We enjoyed browsing through various shops, including a bakery where we bought coffees and date squares to munch on while waiting for the next tourbus.

We proceeded at a mollusk's pace along the very busy, very long Yonge Street. At nearly 2000 kilometres, it was once considered the longest street in the world, until recently. The Pan-American Highway in Central America is now considered the longest. Nevertheless, Yonge Street can still claim distinction as the longest street in Canada. Passing by the University of Toronto, we learned that it is the largest university in Canada. I found out later that Canada has the highest percentage of educated people than any other country—50% having been educated at post-secondary level. Nearby, a vibrant neighbourhood known as The Annex is home to famous Canadian writer Margaret Atwood and other scholarly residents.

Another "not to be missed" neighbourhood was Old Chinatown, where we hopped off just as the skies opened up with an unexpected downpour. Our first stop was a vendor who sold umbrellas, made in China, which strategically leaked, soaking our arms. After several blocks of curio shops and meat markets that all began to look similar, we headed back to the bus stop. Many pedestrians and cyclists seemed oblivious to the rain. Adopting a similar attitude, we re-boarded the bus and decidedly chose to sit on the upper "breezy" level in plastic rain gear issued by our guide.

Thoroughly damp, I was quite relieved to get back to our car. Returning to the QEW, we slowly made our way amidst dense rush-hour traffic back to Burlington. While contemplating our options for dinner and to thaw our chilly bones, I coached Mike on the finer points of making Titanics.

Elly was not impressed that she had to stay at home while we visited the big city. So, I promised that I would take her for a long walk in the woods to make up for it. The next day, we visited Rattlesnake Point on the Niagara Escarpment. Elly bounded down the trail without a care in the world as if she were in her favourite woods back home. *Oh boy, oh boy, I'm on holidays!*

Although Mike had never seen any snakes during previous visits, considering the rocky terrain they are most likely there. Fortunately, we saw none during our two-hour walk on sun-dappled trails. When we came near an unprotected cliff, I put her on leash. In those situations, I'm reminded of a friend who parked his car on top of a five-story building. His exuberant dog jumped out of the back seat and over a low concrete wall, his last willful act.

From several lookouts in the park, a wide valley provided distant views of Burlington as well as rocky cliffs in the Escarpment. Rock climbers were testing their skills in this very popular climbing area, practicing rescue techniques with a stretcher. I was hoping they wouldn't leave before us.

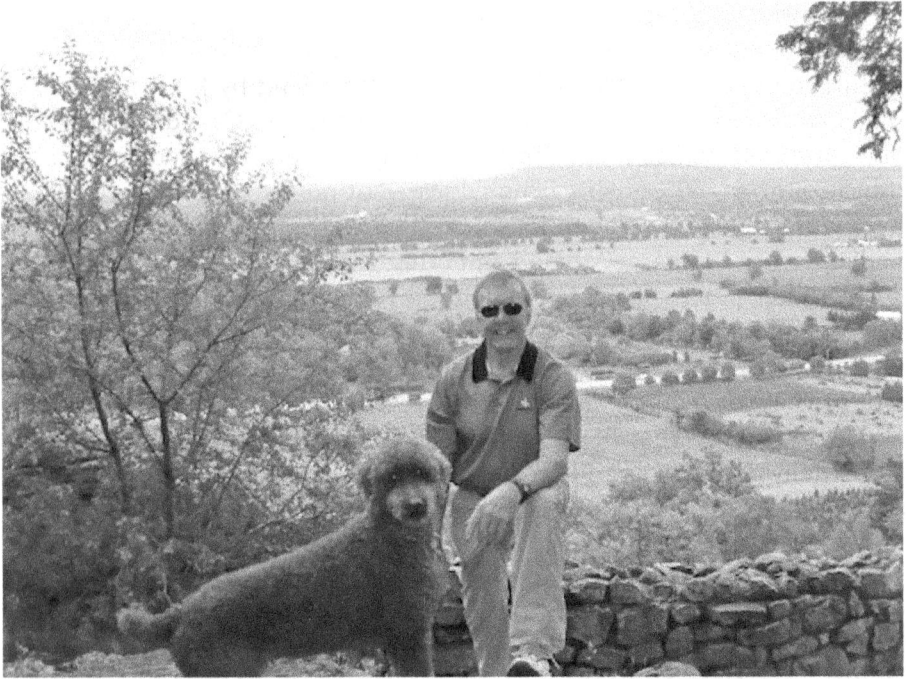

Elly and author at Rattlesnake Point on the Niagara Escarpment, Ontario

Early Saturday morning, we drove south and east on the QEW on our way to Niagara Falls, also known as the "Honeymoon Capital." Numerous Estate Winery signs and extensive vineyards along the highway told us we were in wine country.

Nearing the falls, we noted a tall column on the Escarpment at Queenston Heights, so we decided to check it out. This 56-metre monument marks the grave of Sir Isaac Brock, a legendary war hero and commander of the British Forces of Upper Canada.

In the War of 1812, Brock was killed here leading a charge to repel the American Army who had crossed the Niagara River and captured this strategic Canadian position. Brock's replacement, commander Sheaffe, organized a subsequent attack and was victorious. This pivotal battle lead to a peace treaty signed in 1814 between Britain and the United States, which ultimately defined the territory belonging to Canada.

From war stories to butterflies, the nearby Butterfly Conservatory displays thousands of these delicate creatures flitting about us within a tropical enclosure. Here, we purchased tickets for a bus tour and several popular attractions, including a boat ride on Maid of the Mist and a walk behind the falls. Both provided impressive views of this natural wonder, which drains four of the Great Lakes via the Niagara River into Lake Ontario and eventually into the St. Lawrence River and the Atlantic Ocean.

Two distinct falls are separated by Goat Island: the smaller one belongs to the United States. The larger horseshoe-shaped one belongs to Canada.

One surprising statistic is the rate at which the falls had been eroding the underlying escarpment: 11 kilometres in the past 12,500 years. Recent hydroelectric projects divert some of the water, thereby reducing the amount of erosion from meters to just centimetres per year, ensuring that the falls will remain close to their present location over the next 12,500 years—a comforting thought.

After returning to Burlington, Sandy and I agreed to adopt one of Hedy's two kittens. Our little marmalade orphan with white undercarriage, white face, and blue eyes was originally called "Simon" until his first visit to the vet. Learning that "he" was female, Sandy and Hedy added an "e" to her name.

After a visit to London, Sandy returned with Simone to determine whether Buster and Elly would approve, especially Buster who was normally aggressive with strange cats. We kept the kitten in a cage for a couple of days to help Buster adjust to her odours and behaviours.

While watching carefully, we then allowed both to walk freely about the trailer. Buster mostly ignored her, occasionally hissing and swatting when she got too close. Simone always backed away respectfully, hiding behind a chair or coffee table while keeping an eye on her much bigger brother.

As expected, repeated exposure allowed both of them to learn that neither was a threat. Within a couple of weeks, Simone began stalking Buster, playing with his tail and even jumping on his back. Buster would hiss and run onto the bed or kitchen table when he got tired of her antics.

Elly on the other hand displayed her usual feline fascination, squeaking intermittently day after day as she stalked Simone's every movement. *I can't remember the last time I had this much fun. What is it, the Energizer Bunny?*

After a couple of weeks, she began to settle down with only the occasional squeak, even watching passively as Simone playfully grabbed at her legs.

Elly (10 years) and Simone (10 weeks)

I had hoped this calm demeanour would generalize to other cats but it was not to be. At our next campsite, her obsessive behaviour re-occurred full-blown when a neighbouring cat paraded by as Elly strained at her leash.

For a month or so, Simone's endless curiosity and playful antics had replaced TV as our nightly entertainment. Our first visit to the vet confirmed that she was healthy, tipping the scales at one pound. While traveling, Simone's cage took up half of the back seat, but Elly didn't seem to mind. Often their heads touched through the wire cage as they slept away the kilometres. Buster typically cuddled into his wooly bed on the console between the two front seats.

From Burlington, we headed northeast to Bancroft to visit Sandy's two cousins, whom she hadn't seen in a dozen years. Along the way, we stopped for a few days to reconnect with friends in Lindsay and Bobcaygeon. These towns are located along the historic Trent-Severn Waterway, a canal system that connects lakes and rivers between Lake Ontario and Georgian Bay. Like the Rideau Canal, this waterway has also been designated a National Historic Site operated by Parks Canada.

In Lindsay, a lock keeper told us the locks are opened upon request whenever a boater wishes to be raised or lowered. Because of low bridges and shallow depths, these canals are used mostly by recreational powerboaters. As a sailor, I was aware of the red-right return rule, whereby red markers are always kept on the right side when returning upstream. However, canals present a unique navigational challenge because of a summit about midway. If you were going upstream before the high point, you would be going downstream after. To solve this problem, the red markers are simply switched to the opposite side on the downstream side of the summit, allowing the red-right-return rule to be implemented by all upstream boats, regardless of where they are in the corridor.

Lindsay is a charming little town with a wide main street, angle parking, and rows of hanging flower baskets. A large Inuksuk in its park commemorates a waypoint of the torch relay for the Winter Olympics, recently held in Vancouver in February 2010. A plaque indicates that the torch was carried 45,000 kilometres across Canada, the longest route ever completed by a host country.

Inuksuks (In-uk-shuks) are rock structures used by the Inuit and other Arctic peoples to mark locations of food supplies, productive fishing and hunting areas, or as signposts for travel over barren stretches of tundra. In recent times even in the Arctic wilderness, GPS's have replaced rocks as navigational devices. Consequently, these structures, sometimes shaped like people, tend to be more decorative and whimsical than functional. They can mean whatever people want them to mean.

During our hikes if time and a supply of suitable rocks were available we would build an Inuksuk just for fun, making it as sturdy as possible with the hope that it would still be standing on our next visit. More often than not, we would find a pile of disheveled rocks, possibly the result of a storm or a visit by individuals of the same mentality as those that paint graffiti on rock outcroppings.

Bobcaygeon, which our friend described as "the rockiest place on the planet," has a massive wall of rocks running the entire block along one street. "You can't dig a spade-full of dirt in my yard without finding a rock." Large boulders once considered a nuisance and discarded now appear on nearly every lawn in this community.

In late afternoon, I visited lock 32, one of 45 along the 386-kilometre waterway. Striking up a conversation with a father and son relaxing on a houseboat, I learned that they had rented the craft for a week and that both were novice boaters. I suggested they hang fenders along the side of their boat to protect it from the concrete lock.

"Oh yeah, we forgot" said the son.

I mentioned that we were full-time RVers and briefly described our trip across Canada and wintering in Florida.

The son's eyes glazed over: "I'd like to do the same thing: sell my condo in Toronto and just travel."

"Well, go for it" I said, "I've never met a full-timer who wasn't happy" (I didn't mention that the unhappy ones are no longer full-timing).

"Would you like a beer?" asked the dad, in anticipation of more discourse.

"No thanks, I'm supposed to be shopping and home for dinner shortly."

I wished them a pleasant journey and they did likewise for us. Driving back to the campground, I thought about how many beers I'd been offered from total strangers. I'd lost count.

The morning we were getting ready to leave, our neighbour asked where we were headed. When I said "Bancroft," she remarked, "Say hi to the flies."

Up to this point except in southern Alberta, we hadn't experienced an inordinate number of flies so I made a mental note to enquire about them with the locals. We stopped in Bancroft to buy some lottery tickets, as the prize money of $95 million was then the largest in Canadian history. What is it about large jackpots that encourage people to buy tickets? Certainly, the odds don't change; they're still about the same as being killed by a tornado. Can a prize of $50 million be more valued than a prize of $10 million, or even $1 million? Personally, I think the Lottery Board should take the $95 million and make 95 millionaires, rather than just one multi-millionaire. But then of course, they wouldn't sell as many tickets, so perhaps that's why they haven't asked for my opinion.

Obviously, we didn't win the lottery; otherwise, you wouldn't be reading this. Even though I wasn't writing for financial reasons, I discovered that writing a book is hard work: taking notes, doing research, and re-writing multiple drafts until the words satisfactorily approach reality. According to Steinbeck, he kept most of his notes in his head and some time later put them to paper. My head is not quite big enough to hold more than two notes, so I used a digital recorder, usually transcribing them into printed words within a week. I found the absolute worst part of writing is waking up in the middle of the night with a thought about how to best describe a particular aspect of our journey. Initially, I kept my recorder beside the bed and just start dictating, which only lasted until the first time I woke Sandy.

"What are you doing?" she mumbled.

"I'm dictating a paragraph about our trip."

"Well," she replied slightly perturbed, "Can you dictate in the living room? You woke me up."

Obviously, she didn't need to add that second part. From then on, when inspiration struck I would get up and go into the living room to put my thoughts together, sometimes with a little nip or two to stimulate the brain cells, and then go back to bed. Too often before falling back to sleep, I would think of a slightly better way to relate a story and get up another two or three times to re-dictate. Did I say that writing a book is hard work? It's even harder when you're anal-retentive and sleep deprived!

In the process of this endeavour, I've garnered a new appreciation for prolific authors like Steinbeck. The overleaf of *Travels with Charley* lists ten fiction, eight nonfiction, two plays, and various collections of literary works that he produced in his illustrious career. I doubt that John wrote mainly for financial compensation although I wonder how productive he would have been if he had won the lottery early in his career. Maybe authors shouldn't be allowed to buy lottery tickets? No...bad idea!

Sandy's cousin Dianne and her husband Harry have a 200-acre farm just north of Bancroft. Both are retired so the farm is not a source of income—just a hobby with a few cows and chickens. We parked in their driveway for several days while they showed us their acreage and the local area. Elly played with their Australian Shepherd occasionally stopping to sniff and pace. *I know there's a cat around here; I can smell it, and I won't relax until I track it down.*

Being a wizened outdoor cat, he never showed himself while Elly was around. Eventually, she settled on a rug by the door while we visited inside.

To view their acreage, we doubled up on quads, also known as four-wheelers—a bit noisy for my liking, but exhilarating. Harry escorted us across fields and into the forest to their "sugar shack" where they make maple syrup.

During March each year when the temperature hovers around freezing, they tap into a couple of hundred maple trees, all at least ten inches in diameter. The sap is collected in pails and poured into a stainless-steel vat, where it is then transferred to a large flat pan atop a wood-fired stove. Boiling the sap removes water through evaporation. It's a slow process: about ten gallons of sap is required to make one gallon of syrup. Continued boiling results in maple-butter spread and finally, candy. Sometimes, they'll pour syrup on a clean snow bank and eat it immediately as maple taffy, a traditional treat at maple-syrup festivals, quite common in northern Ontario and Quebec. In full production, Harry said he stays overnight near the stove to ensure the sap is not overheated: "At a critical point in the process, it wouldn't take much to burn the whole batch."

For breakfast, we poured their syrup on waffles, savouring the rich maple flavour. Afterward, we attended a church service with Dianne and Harry where I took the opportunity to bring up the question of flies with a local gentleman.

"Some years they can be bad about now — horse flies, house flies, deer flies, black flies, and no-see-ums — but this year they're not a problem because the unusually hot weather in April caused them to hatch early." He continued, "the no-see-ums are so small, they can go right through screens; and they bite, leaving a small red mark that itches." Since you can actually see these little critters, I wondered why they're called no-see-ums, and whether Buster would stalk them like he does houseflies.

Later that day, we all visited Sandy's other cousin Donna and her husband Claude who live on a lake in Bancroft. Dianne, Sandy, and I spent a sunshiny day cruising slowly around the lake in a three-person paddleboat. A pair of loons, often seen in Canada's lakes, observed us cautiously in one quiet bay. Two baby chicks were riding on the mother's back. A similar sense of family prevailed in both cousins' homes, evidenced by framed photos of kids and grand kids adorning every wall. Their fridges looked like pinup boards with notes, photos, and grandkid's drawings, so commonly found in close-knit families.

Harry drove us through a maze of dirt roads crisscrossing the heavily treed countryside. I asked what the rock outcroppings were called beside the roads here on the eastern edge of the Canadian Shield. Having grown up in the area, he said that whenever a vehicle accidentally crashes into them, the newspaper calls them "rock cuts."

We browsed through shops displaying local art and pottery in nearby Maynooth, followed by dinner at a popular restaurant. Harry and Dianne both had commitments the next day, so we said our good-byes and headed east toward Ottawa. As a going away gift, they gave us a large jar of their homemade maple syrup and another of maple butter, which we cherished the entire trip.

A week later, we stopped at a popular bakery in Quebec and purchased some stone-ground whole wheat bread with sesame seeds. When toasted and topped with maple butter, it was very likely the best thing I'd ever eaten. In a subsequent phone call, Dianne was delighted to hear that I was enjoying it immensely.

Closer to Ottawa, the mostly rocky bush was replaced by green fields of grain, with the occasional dairy and cattle farm. We booked six nights at a nearby campground, giving us sufficient time to fully explore the Capital of Canada. Since the truck needed an oil change, I made an early appointment at a downtown dealership that kindly provided us with a ride to the Canadian Museum of Civilization, "worth seeing" according to our friend in Bobcaygeon. This ultra-modern building is located directly across the Ottawa River in Gatineau, Quebec, previously known as Hull. Here, we spent hours reading placards and listening to audio recordings describing 25 significant individuals who helped shape our nation.

Based on my wanderlust inclinations, I was enamoured with David Thompson, an explorer and cartographer who spent nearly 30 years mapping the remoteness of western Canada. Simon Fraser, a contemporary fur trader, named BC's Thompson River in his honour. Thompson returned the favour by attaching his friend's name to the majestic river we had visited earlier, the Fraser River. During his early retirement, Thompson wrote an account of his findings *Travels in Western North America, 1784-1812*, but was unable to find a publisher during his remaining years. Although he died destitute in 1857, his work was published posthumously and is now considered a classic. A thick bound copy was on display in a glass case at the museum, which lead me to wonder whether writers would be better off financially focusing on just one monumental book or numerous, less significant books in the hopes of publishing at least something? I'm more inclined to favour the latter approach, rather than dying destitute.

On another floor of the museum, we meandered through a litany of artifacts, depicting 1000 years of Canadian history through life-size reconstructions. Days, rather than hours, would have been a more appropriate time allotment to fully appreciate these exhibits.

Shortly after noon, the floor and walls began shaking vigorously, accompanied by a thunderous sound. At first, I thought it might be special effects from a nearby exhibit. However, as the shaking became more pronounced, I reassessed it as an earthquake and positioned myself underneath a door frame. Other patrons looked alarmed, but everyone managed to stay calm. Within 20 seconds, the shaking stopped. A security guard mentioned that it was indeed an earthquake. The evening news reported it as the strongest quake to hit the Ottawa area in 21 years, magnitude 5.0, with its epicentre just 25 kilometres away. Fortunately, there were no injuries and minimal damage, although some government buildings had been temporarily evacuated.

On our second day, we took a bus tour of the city to learn more about various points of interest. Ottawa's most prominent landmark is its Gothic-style Parliament Building, built in 1866 on a hill overlooking the confluence of the Ottawa River and Rideau Canal. Its massive stonewalls, majestic towers, and green copper roofs provide the centrepiece of Canadian democracy.

Parliament Building overlooking Ottawa River in Ottawa, Ontario

Other government buildings, foreign embassies, museums, monuments, and statues are around every corner. Our tour guide mentioned that most employees in the region, about 80%, work for the government. Twenty thousand government employees work in just one building, second only to the Pentagon in the United States.

We passed by 24 Sussex Drive, home of Canada's Prime Minister. Our guide mentioned its appraised value at six million. That seemed pricey until we passed by 1 Sussex Drive, home of the Governor General. Its value was ten times as much, likely due to the extensive, meticulously maintained property. Unlike the Prime Minister's home, Rideau Hall is open for viewing by the public.

Later that day, we took a guided walking tour of Parliament where the House of Commons and the Senate conduct their meetings. The recently renovated Library of Parliament, used only by politicians, was most impressive. According to our guide, it is the only section of the Parliament building that was spared from destruction by a fire in 1916, simply because a guard had the foresight to close its steel-door entryway when the alarm sounded.

Outside on the grounds is a small building housing feral cats that are free to come and go. A sign indicates that a volunteer relies on public donations for their care, so we contributed on behalf of Elly. When we returned to the campground, Elly seemed quite intrigued with my description of the cattery, tilting her head from side to side: *Did you see any cats?* "Yes, we saw one eating and several sleeping." *Maybe I can get to go to the Parliament grounds tomorrow instead of babysitting my brother and sister? Can I please?* I fibbed to her that they don't allow dogs on Parliament Hill ... they actually do, on leash.

The next day, we took a boat tour on the Ottawa River, which played a significant role in the development of our country. Early explorers, fur traders, and pioneers traveled this waterway from the St. Lawrence River to reach the heart of the Capital region. The intersecting Rideau Canal was built in the early 1800's as an alternate route to access the Capital from Lake Ontario, or vice versa. Eight short locks, within the length of a city block, lower recreational boats 24 metres from the Rideau Canal into the River, a two-hour process. A monument is dedicated to the thousand workers, mostly Irish immigrants, who died during the six years it took to construct this waterway. In winter, the section of the Canal passing through central Ottawa becomes the world's longest skating rink, nearly 8 kilometres in length.

Nearly everyone we met in Ottawa spoke both French and English, the two official languages in Canada. Sandy, who had taken several years of French in high school, was delighted to reacquaint herself with the language. I, on the other hand, had a limited knowledge of French acquired mostly by reading the back of cereal boxes, printed in both languages. Thus, I had no difficulty saying "Cheerios" or "Raisin Bran." However, after breakfast, I was finished talking for the day! Street signs are also in both languages, similar to the French quarter of Winnipeg.

Flags fly everywhere in Ottawa, not only Canadian flags atop most significant buildings, but foreign flags identifying 135 foreign embassies in the city. Physical exercise was very popular...a plethora of bicyclists, rollerbladers, runners, and walkers made good use of an extensive ribbon of paved paths bordering both the canal and the river.

Near the Parliament building, we paid our respects at the Tomb of the Unknown Soldier, where a solemn ceremony occurs on Remembrance

Day, November 11th, honouring the thousands of soldiers who died in Canada's various wars, including WWI, WWII, and the Korean war. Sadly, an addition to the monument will honour those who died in the current war in Afghanistan. Since we drove along the Highway of Heroes near Toronto just 60 days ago, another eight Canadians had been killed in this conflict, bringing the total to 150. We left the monument feeling optimistic that Canada will abide by its stated commitment to withdraw troops in the summer of 2011.

A few blocks away on York Street is one of the largest open air markets in the world, the By Ward Market, where buskers entertain, farmers and artisans sell their wares in makeshift tents, and patrons relax and enjoy gastronomic delights on sidewalk patios. After lunching at a French bakery, we bought a couple of "Obama cookies," named after the US president, who had stopped by last year while on a visit to Ottawa. He saw the shortbread cookies decorated with a maple leaf and purchased some for his children. According to our bus-tour guide, the bakery had been selling about 70 cookies a week prior to the president's visit. After labeling them and posting a photo of Obama beside the cookies, sales increased to over 1000 a week.

I wondered if our Prime Minister Steven Harper had purchased cookies with an American flag logo in Washington D.C., whether there would be an increase in sales of "Harper cookies." Not likely! Having lived and traveled extensively in both countries, I'm always somewhat embarrassed at how little Americans seem to know about Canada, compared to Canadians' knowledge of the United States. Just during our past winter in Florida, I was asked: "Are the Vancouver Olympics being held in Canada? What's your current president's name? Do the Colorado Rockies go as far north as Canada? What's it like living in Canada?" And these were all serious enquires of adults, not fifth graders!

On our last day in Ottawa, we browsed the National Gallery of Canada, which houses the largest collection of Canadian art in the world from aboriginal beadwork to modern day abstract and pop art. It was my first exposure to a collection of original paintings by Canadian artists known as the "Group of Seven."

In the early 1900's, these Torontonian artists focused on capturing landscapes, mostly along the Canadian Shield in northern Ontario. They sketched outdoors in oil on small pads, later transferring the images to larger canvases back in their city studios. As indicated in an information booklet, their colourful paintings illustrate a "decorative approach to the vast Canadian terrain."

Outside the Gallery's entrance, a gigantic sculpture of a spider attracted the attention of visitors, especially school children who wanted to be photographed underneath the bug. Our tour guide said, almost apologetically, that the sculpture cost over three million dollars to construct. There was little in Ottawa to suggest that our country was in the midst of a global recession. Fortunately, partly a result of our bountiful resources and sound fiscal policies, we were less affected by the current economic downturn than many other countries, including our neighbour to the south.

Larry MacDonald, Ph.D.

6

QUEBEC

"JE ME SOUVIENS"

Saying on Quebec license plates

We left Ontario none too soon. After three months our provincial map had become worn and torn on the creases, resembling Venetian blinds, with penciled circles showing campsites and yellow highlighter tracing routes. Crossing the border onto Route 40, we stopped at an Information Centre to obtain a map of Quebec and a French-English phrase book. Sandy did most of the talking, some *en Français*, to the bilingual agent who advised us of the best route through Montreal to our campground on the eastern outskirts.

Quebec's roads were reminiscent of those near Winnipeg—rough, especially the side roads. So rough that Simone got airtime from her blanket, Andy bounced across the dashboard, and a plastic cover on the bottom rear section of the trailer broke away from its screws and was seriously hanging down when we got to the campground. I reattached it by fastening metal strips to the yet unbroken plastic, the only major repair I had to make to either vehicle on our entire trip.

Montreal, the second largest city in Canada, is an island bordered by two lakes and two rivers, the most prominent one being the St. Lawrence. From our campground, we took a shuttle bus to a downtown depot where we boarded a "hop on-hop off" tour bus. Our two-hour tour covered over 200 points of interest, but we only got off twice: to visit the St Joseph Oratory atop prominent Mount Royal and again to check out Rue St Catherine (St Catherine Street) which, according to our guide, is the longest commercial street in the world, 11 kilometres. Beneath it is also the largest underground shopping complex in the world, although, as someone who detests shopping, I'm happy to report that we never found the entrance.

The Oratory's domed basilica is the largest in Canada, seating 2,200 people with standing room for 10,000 more. In the early 1900's its founder, Brother Andrè, reportedly performed many healing miracles, evidenced by the used crutches and thank-you notes on display. When Andrè died in 1937, his heart was placed on display in a glass urn, an ancient custom in France where the hearts of kings were displayed as a sign of admiration. During our visit, several people were seeking miracles by laboriously climbing on their knees up 256 stairs toward the basilica, praying briefly on each step.

Back on the bus, we enjoyed a stunning view of Montreal and the St. Lawrence River from Mount Royal. The nearby mountainous community of Westmount reportedly has some of the highest-priced real estate in Canada. Brian Mulroney, a former Prime Minister, lives there. We had just enough time for lunch before catching the shuttle back to our campground.

Earlier in the week, we had arranged to meet our friends, Ian and Judy, who live in Montreal. This time, we took the Metro, an extensive underground railway that transports people throughout the city. A colour-coded map with identified stations makes it very user friendly. Parking on the south shore of the St. Lawrence, we boarded the train which whisked us quietly along to a central station. From there, we transferred to another train for a short ride to Place Jacque Cartier in Old Montreal. This historic square, lined with patios and decorated with colourful flowers, was overflowing with visitors being entertained by street buskers. According to Ian, the founder of Cirque du Soleil got his start here, entertaining tourists many years ago.

Together with dozens of people, we jostled through a narrow alleyway that provided a venue for enterprising artists selling their creations. At Sailor's Church, where early mariners came to pray before and after their voyages, miniature wooden sailing vessels hung from the ceiling. We then drove to Olympic Park, site of the 1976 Summer Olympics.

The inclined tower of Olympic Stadium is apparently the tallest of its kind, 175 metres; unfortunately, the Stadium's removable roof had developed substantial leaks and replacement costs were estimated at several million dollars. Since it was no longer being used for major sporting events, our friends suggested it be torn down. My counter-suggestion was to tear down the unused stadium but retain the inclined tower as a symbol of the Olympics. Perhaps a referendum would resolve this issue, since Montrealers would be picking up the tab.

From the east end of Montreal, we drove to Lachine ("China" in French), a suburb on the west end. A stone warehouse built in 1803 to store furs is now a museum containing artifacts and stories of the thriving fur industry during the 18th and 19th centuries. According to a plaque beside the Lachine Canal, this land was deeded to de La Salle, a French explorer, and named by his detractors to belittle his dream of finding a route to China. The canal allowed fur traders to circumvent a set of treacherous rapids in the St. Lawrence River. Later, dredging of the river made the canal obsolete, although picnickers, bikers, and sightseers were enjoying its green banks and well-kept pathways.

We arranged to spend a few days with Judy and Ian at their country home in the Eastern Townships, an area of rolling hills, lakes, and forests, a short distance southeast from Montreal. With Sherbrooke as its hub, this area offers a weekend retreat for Montrealers, as evidenced by bumper-to-bumper traffic returning to the city late Sunday afternoon.

Their home is near the charming hamlet of Georgeville, population 49, on the shore of Lake Memphre Magog. "Memphre" takes its name from the legendary sea creature that reportedly lives within the waters of the second largest lake in Quebec. We parked the trailer for several days in their driveway giving us an opportunity to visit Abbaye de Saint-Benoit-du-Lac (Abbey of Saint Benoit of the Lake), a monastery where Benedictine monks have lived a contemplative religious life since 1912. An attached store sells products made by the monks, including apple cider, cheese curds, and chocolate, all of which were very tasty. During our stay, Ian and I played a round of golf at Jay Peak Resort just across the border in Vermont, and another at a local course in Georgeville.

Our next stop was a campground in Compton, still in the Eastern Townships. After unhooking the trailer, we drove to the small village of Coaticook, which has the longest walking suspension bridge in the world, 169 metres, according to the Guinness Book of Records. The bridge had closed for the day, which suited Elly just fine: *If you've walk one suspension bridge, you've walked them all.*

As we drove about the rural countryside, Sandy reacted with enthusiastic joy at the well maintained farmhouses with wide front porches, landscaped lawns, and flower gardens. The appearance and smells of farmyards reminded her of youthful summers spent on her Uncle's farm in Ontario. Elly had numerous opportunities to "look at the cows." Since I hadn't told Elly about the difference between cows and steers, she saw them as all alike—just like her dad.

A local dairy sold Anciennes Crème Glacee (old fashioned ice cream), which we agreed was the best of our entire trip. We stopped again at a farmer's market where Sandy practiced her French while the owner practiced her English.

An hour later, we purchased a couple of tomatoes. Our brief visit to the Townships did not allow visiting the many natural and historical attractions within this scenic region of southeastern Quebec. So much to see, so little time.

A three-hour drive took us to a campground in Lévis (pronounced Levy) just across the St. Lawrence River from historic Quebec City. The next day we parked the truck and took a ten-minute ferry ride across the river. Hearing most passengers speaking French and seeing majestic Chateau Frontenac perched high on a promontory with its brick façade, tall spirals, and green roof, Sandy commented, "I feel like I'm in Europe."

Chateau Frontenac in Quebec City with Quebec flag in foreground

After disembarking, we became immediately enthralled by the narrow cobblestone streets, 18th Century architecture, and bustling outdoor patios. A lineup of tourists waiting for the "funicular," a cable car that hauls people up steep inclines, prompted us to hike up the angled streets and staircases to our tour-bus station on top of the promontory.

At the top, a crowd surrounded a busker doing tricks on tiny bicycles, one not much bigger than a roller skate. Summer Festival was occurring in Quebec City, allowing us to see many entertainers during our visit.

On a two-hour bus tour through Quebec City, our guide provided commentary about the city's 400-year history, including several significant buildings and monuments. A statue of Champlain, similar to the one we had seen in Ottawa, stood beside Hotel Frontenac in honour of the French explorer who founded Quebec City in 1608. Nearly 150 years later because of the city's strategic location overlooking the St. Lawrence River, Britain laid claim to the city after defeating the French on the Plains of Abraham.

On September 13, 1759 under the cover of darkness, British soldiers climbed up steep cliffs using roots and tree branches as hand holds, to engage the French Army encamped above. In less than half an hour, the main battle was over with the British general Wolfe and the French general Montcalm both mortally wounded. Hundreds of soldiers were killed or wounded, three times as many French as British. Three years later, after another French army attempted unsuccessfully to regain control of Quebec City, France officially ceded its Canadian territories to England. Today, the Plains of Abraham stand in silent testament to these strategic battles that shaped the destiny of Canada.

Massive walls several kilometres in length surround the old town, making it the only walled city in North America. They served well to repel the Americans, including Generals Richard Montgomery and Benedict Arnold in 1775 and again in the war of 1812. To protect the city against future invaders, the British built a 37-acre, star-shaped fortress known as the Citadel, completed in 1831, which still functions today as an active military garrison for the Royal 22e Regiment. Charles Dickens, in his *American Notes* of 1842, dubbed the walled city and its cliffs "The Gibraltar of America."

After our tour, we dined at an authentic Quebec restaurant, which offered a traditional French dessert of Maple Syrup Pie with dollops of whipped cream. We justified our gluttonous ways by walking to the Notre-Dame de Quebec Basilica, then to several art galleries, and finally through a crowded alley where local artists displayed their paintings. After walking down the stairway to the lower city, we stopped at a bistro patio for a cool one while listening to a classical guitarist who should be famous. Quebec City reeks with romantic ambience.

That evening, we watched the Image Mill, advertised as "The world's largest outdoor multimedia show." Projected nightly on a row of silos at Old Port Mill, the images depict the history of Quebec City. Afterwards, the 11:30 pm ferry, packed with reveling tourists, provided our ride back to Lévis.

The next day, instead of taking the ferry, we drove to Quebec City. Dining high above the city in a rotating restaurant gave us a bird's-eye view of the downtown area and surrounding countryside. Afterwards, we visited monuments marking the locations where the two opposing generals, Wolfe and Montcalm, had died on the Plains of Abraham. A prominent plaque noted that this now peaceful plateau was named after Abraham Martin, a shepherd who once tended his flocks here. A bronze statue of horse-mounted Joan of Arc, commemorating the battles of 1759-60, was the centrepiece of a beautiful flower-filled park.

Santayana, a well-known musician, was playing on one of the outdoor stages later that evening. But we chose instead to watch a free showing of Cirque du Soleil in an unlikely setting—beneath a freeway bridge. Dozens of costumed performers displayed amazing stunts and acrobatics, entertaining an appreciative crowd. Both shows finished at the same time, resulting in hordes of happy people overflowing the sidewalks. After two days and two nights of nonstop pleasure, we were ready for some downtime, which meant moving to a new destination.

In 2009, National Geographic Society designated the Gaspé Peninsula as the third most beautiful destination in the world, after the Norwegian Fjords and Kootenay/Yoho National Parks in British Columbia. It encompasses a string of picturesque coastal villages along 800 kilometres of Highway 132 beside the St. Lawrence River and Gulf.

While in Quebec, we had asked quite a few campers whether we could take the trailer around the Peninsula. Some said we could and definitely should, as the countryside was strikingly beautiful. Others alleged that the narrow roads and steep hills would be difficult to negotiate because of our length. For me, that only added to the challenge. Since campgrounds were liberally scattered along the route, we decided to give it a go, and were glad we did since this side trip was one of the highlights of our travels.

On our first leg to Riviére-du-Loup, we visited the small town of Kamouraska, home to two prominent Canadians: Adolphe Basile Routhier who penned the lyrics of our national anthem "Oh Canada," and René Chaloult who designed the Quebec flag. We kept our eyes peeled for a Victorian-style home converted to a bakery that advertised breads made with "whole grain flower, stone-milled to guarantee freshness and nutritive value." The bread was very tasty, especially when toasted and topped with Dianne's maple-butter spread.

During our two-day stay at a campground, I spoke with our French neighbour about the meaning of the saying on Quebec license plates. He answered with a grin: "I'm not sure. The plates used to say LA BELLE PROVINCE (beautiful province), which made sense to me. Then, some bureaucrat decided to change it to JE ME SOUVIENS (I remember), but I'm not sure what I'm supposed to remember!"

His reply prompted me to conduct a brief survey while in Quebec: we asked a random sample of ten French Canadians what this new saying meant to them. Half were uncertain about what they were expected to remember, suggesting vague notions about tenuous relationships between the French and the English. The other half said in essence that they should remember their heritage—their history and traditions—and be proud to be French. Obviously, Quebecers would benefit from receiving information about the intended meaning of this saying, perhaps annually when license plates are renewed.

After two days, we departed Riviére-du-Loup onto Route des Navigateurs (Route of the Navigators), a two-lane roadway that connects a series of villages along the coastline of the St. Lawrence River. Each town's church steeple, adorned in gleaming silver, could be seen protruding above the landscape long before we entered the town-site. The gently rolling highway between shoreline and mountains provided breathtaking views, most of which were behind us by the time Sandy got out the camera. We often had to pass by scenic overlooks and picnic areas because they were either too small or too crowded to access with our rig. Appropriate signage RV ACCESSIBLE would have been helpful, in both languages of course.

The town of Rimouski had no significance to us at the time. Later however at a maritime museum in Halifax, Nova Scotia, we learned that the worst maritime disaster in Canada occurred in the St. Lawrence River just off shore here. On May 29, 1914, two years after the Titanic disaster, the Empress of Ireland with 1500 aboard was hit broadside by a coal-carrying freighter in fog. Millions of gallons of water poured through the gaping hole in its hull. Over 1000 died, many from hypothermia. Imagine the sheer terror of these people scrambling to escape first the ship, and then the freezing water as the Empress turned turtle and sank within fifteen minutes!

We had made reservations at a campground in Cap Chat (Cape Cat), which was Elly's idea of the perfect destination. When we arrived, she inquired: *OK, I see the Cape, but where's the Cat?*

I told her the town was named after a rock formation and that I would take a picture of it to show her. I did—she was not impressed. *How do you chase a rock?*

Our campsite fronted a rocky beach along the St. Lawrence, reminding us so much of the west coast: tidal changes, worn rocks dressed in algae, sea gulls, sailboats, and the ubiquitous smell of the sea, or more accurately, decaying seaweed. It smelled like home.

A vast collection of turbine wind generators came into view on a mountaintop as we approached the Cape. I wondered whether the environmental concerns of blade noise and bird kills reported in southern Alberta would be similar here.

After unhooking the trailer at our campsite, we stopped for a tour of Eole, named after the Greek God of Wind. Our guide took us inside the largest vertical-axis wind turbine in the world; build as a prototype in 1986 but no longer operating. He also discussed features of the 76 horizontal-axis wind turbines, those we had seen earlier, each producing enough energy for 4000 homes. In response to my questions, he replied: "To my knowledge, no birds have been killed by the blades and they make about as much noise as the rustling of leaves."

After our tour, Sandy and I walked to the base of one of the giant propellers turning steadily in a stiff breeze. Weighing 37 tons and standing 55 metres high, it was definitely noisier than rustling leaves, but since no one lived nearby, what did it matter? Our guide said the newer and taller turbines, the one's we would see later on the Gaspé Peninsula, were quieter still. We looked about the base for dead birds, but found none.

N\nmmmmmmmmmmmmmmmmmmmmmmmmmmmmmmm
\\\\\\\\\\\\\\\\\\\\\\\\\ *f*†††≥ç *f*≥≥

While we were having dinner, Simone added her cryptic comments by strolling across my laptop. She probably figured if Elly could make comments during our travels, she could too!

The province of Quebec is the largest producer of hydro-electricity in Canada, aided by its many rivers and mountainous typography. In fact,

Canada has more lakes and rivers than all other countries in the world combined, offering tremendous potential for producing clean energy.

As environmentalists, we liked what we saw here: in addition to the wind farms were crystal clear streams and rivers world renown for their salmon, robust green forests, wide-shouldered roads to accommodate bicyclists, grocery stores charging for plastic bags, plentiful recycling bins in towns and campgrounds, and numerous displays of laundry hanging outside to dry.

"Construction Holidays" in Quebec are the last two weeks in July, designated for construction workers to take time off. Reportedly, about 40% of Quebecers take their holidays during this time, which explained why we were unable to remain in our Cap Chat campground for an additional day—our site had been reserved.

During these two weeks, we decided to always phone ahead to ensure availability. No problem: our first reservation was confirmed near the town of Gaspé. Along the way, evergreen-blanketed mountainsides showed no evidence of clear-cutting or pine-beetle damage like we witnessed in British Columbia. A number of homes had unique ski-slope roofs. Uncertain as to why, I guessed that they help retain snow in the winter for insulation purposes, but none of the locals seemed to know. A conspicuous characteristic of most properties in the Gaspé Peninsula was the meticulously mown and landscaped yards. People here were proud of home ownership and it showed.

We passed through Cap-des-Rosiers (Cape of the Roses), named after the plentiful roses growing along the Cape. It is home of the tallest lighthouse in Canada, which projects a powerful beacon over 40 meters above the sea. It was on this cape that the British ship carrying General Wolfe was spotted in 1759, prompting a message being sent to French Forces in Quebec City—not that it mattered. The Micmac Indians, early inhabitants of this eastern-most point of the Gaspé Peninsula, called the area Gaspeg, meaning "end of the land." It also marks the demarcation line between the St. Lawrence River and the Gulf of St. Lawrence.

Our campground near the town of Gaspé overlooked the bay where French explorer Jacques Cartier landed on July 24, 1534 and claimed Canada for France. A monument and massive stone cross commemorate this historic event. Later arrivals included the English, Irish, Scottish, and other nationalities that created the traditions and cultures still evident today in the varied architecture, accents, and culinary delights of the region.

It was here we befriended a young French couple, each of us struggling to use the other's language. Their two school-age children had a look of amazement on their faces when they learned that I could not count to ten in French, but I could tell them *en francais* my favourite cereal!

Their parents generously provided us with a container of homemade soup, and we in turn gave the children a French/English book about the 2010 Vancouver Olympics mascots. The young boy expressed his delight in English: "Thank you very, very, very, very, very much."

Sandy replied: "Tres, tres, tres, tres, tres bienvenue." We all had a good laugh.

By coincidence, we continued to meet up with this family at two other campgrounds during our final week in Quebec. Sandy, always the teacher, made sure they both learned some English while she in turn learned some French. A few more gift exchanges occurred, almost as if we both wanted to be the last presenter. They won, dropping off a package of salted pork belly to go with the soup recipe. We didn't have the heart to tell them that Sandy is a vegetarian and that I've got an aversion to pork bellies, salted or otherwise.

They were delighted to see our poodle (in French, Caniche Royale) perform tricks such as singing Happy Birthday and saying bedtime prayers. When Elly was younger, I taught her to pray by sitting upright with her front legs on my horizontal thigh. On cue, "Pray," she would lower her face between her crossed legs and wait while one of us recited: "Now I lay me down to sleep, I hope I wake up to a treat. Amen." She would then raise her head, usually to applause from adults and squeals of delight from children. Of course, we would immediately give her a treat as well, which is probably what she prayed for. *In French, I'm called a Caniche Royale, which I find a lot classier than Standard Poodle. Maybe we can move to Quebec some day?*

"Not likely," I replied, "at least not until I can count to ten!"

Having a friendly dog, even if she didn't speak French, helped facilitate positive relationships with many of the people we met along the way. Steinbeck found the same during his travels with Charley.

On several occasions before arriving in Quebec, we were given notice, "French people are standoffish." They were not so with us. We were repeatedly impressed with their friendliness and willingness to engage in conversation. Our awkward attempts to speak French and copious amounts of laughter always seemed to bring out a reciprocal response, no doubt paving the way for a positive encounter.

From Gaspé, we continued our journey along the shoreline with spectacular views of the St. John River, Gaspé Bay, and the Gulf of St. Lawrence. Nearing our next destination, we descended a steep grade (17% for a kilometre) leading into the very busy village of Percé where traffic came to a standstill as groups of tourists scurried across the road.

Others browsed through an array of trendy shops and art galleries, or clustered around posted restaurant menus trying to decide where to eat.

Percé derives its name from an arc-shaped hole at sea level piercing a massive cathedral of limestone, Percé Rock, which juts up from the ocean just offshore. Early explorers wrote that they could sail their ship through it, although I doubt that any tried. This rock reminded us of similar-shaped geological formations we had seen in the Bay of Islands, New Zealand and in Cabo San Lucas, Mexico. Excursion boats, lining the quay, provided tourists with a close-up look at the famous rock as well as nearby Bonaventure Island, home to the largest colony of Gannet seabirds in North America.

Percé Rock near the town of Percé on Gaspé Peninsula, Quebec

Our campground was situated on a bluff with a potential view of the archway from our rear window. Unfortunately, the owner of an adjacent B&B took advantage of the breezy, sunny day by hanging out some large bed sheets that blocked our view for the entire first day. We were camped close enough that we walked to this picturesque community, purchased some long overdue "Thank You" cards, and dined with a quayside view of tour boats and passengers coming and going.

On a 3-hour drive winding along the southern shore of Gaspé Peninsula, we passed through New Carlisle, the hometown of René Levesque, Premier of Quebec between 1976 and 1985. His statue and platitudes are presumably located in the municipal park although a lack of nearby parking prevented us from stopping. Levesque's major political achievement was establishing and heading the Parti Québécois party, which promoted the notion that Quebec should become a sovereign nation separate from Canada. Proponents were called "Separatists." However, provincial referendums on this issue in 1980 and again in 1995 were defeated, albeit narrowly.

Over the ensuing years, the relationship between staunch Canadians and French Separatists, who are also Canadians, has been slow to mend. Even today, as one Quebecer told us, "It is a see-saw balancing act between Anglophones and Francophones that carries over into everyday life. Although separation is no longer a political issue, there are still some who would like to see it happen." With a change in leadership, both federally and provincially, this issue has taken a back seat to the more pressing concerns of a slumping economy. Sandy and I developed a fondness for Quebec and hoped that these warm and hospitable people will always consider themselves Canadians first, Quebecers second.

The green highlands of New Brunswick could be seen across the shimmering expanse of the Baie de Chaleurs (Bay of Warmth). Brochures describe the water as the warmest north of Virginia Beach.

From our campground at Carleton-sur-Mer, we walked barefoot in the water, concluding that "warm" is a relative term—swimming was out of the question, which was fine with Elly. However, an extensive blacktop trail skirting the water's edge enticed me to exercise by roller blading, while practicing my bonjours to everyone along the way. Replies ranged from "bonjour" to I didn't have a clue.

From our rear window facing a shallow lagoon, we observed a seagull dropping a clamshell from a height around 10 metres onto the rocks below, and immediately diving down after it. This problem-solving behaviour was identical to that we had seen on the west coast. If the shell broke open, the gull would eat the clam. If not, the bird would drop it again and again until the shell broke. I often wondered how they acquire this behaviour. Is it learned? Do adult birds show their fledglings where to find the shells, how high to fly before dropping them, and how to ensure they land on rocks rather than sand? This complex behaviour appears to be as natural and universal as soaring in the wind. Perhaps it's instinctive? My readings on the subject of "instincts," however, extensively researched by psychologist Frank Beach, suggest that such behaviours do not occur in the absence of early experiences.

While it was generally thought that female rats build nests "instinctively" before giving birth, Beach demonstrated that they fail to do so if deprived of opportunities to manipulate nest-like materials, including their tails, earlier in their lives. In the case of gulls, I often wonder what early experiences are required to ensure they break open clamshells by dropping them on rocks.

As I write this, I notice that our kitten is busy trying to capture a fly that had gotten into the trailer. Buster chases flies; so does Simone. Assuming this behaviour is not "instinctive," what early experiences might be required for its occurrence? Certainly, they both have had extensive experience carrying stuffed toys in their mouths and manipulating their tails. Would they chase flies if they had been deprived of such experiences? Early in my career as a research psychologist, I would have been keen to conduct a study to answer that question. Now, I don't really care, as long as they are enjoying themselves and in the process, keeping the fly population at bay.

Steady onshore winds provided ideal conditions for local kite surfers, sailing back and forth near the entrance to the lagoon. Propelling themselves skyward off small waves and landing gently in the water, they skimmed along at high speeds and rakish angles. I spoke to one young lad who seemed to be having difficulties keeping his large kite aloft. "I've been practicing for five days and still don't have the 'hang' of it." I'm sure he was totally unaware of the pun! "Hang in there," I replied with a wry smile, as we left for an early dinner at a nearby restaurant.

That evening, we attended a Kenny Rogers concert at nearby New Richmond, the first time the Quebec Summer Festival had been held outside of Quebec City. Several thousand people stood shoulder-to-shoulder, singing and swaying along to "Lucile" and "The Gambler." We were surprised that a performer of Kenny's stature would be entertaining in such an out-of-the-way place. Although he was the headliner, the mostly French audience was even more enthralled with the warm-up singer, Laurence Jalbert, a well-known local talent. This woman's powerful voice and energetic movements were very entertaining, even if we didn't understand the words—sort of a female Mike Jagger.

Exotic Quebec captivated our minds and our souls with its natural beauty and hospitable people. But it was time to break free from its magical spell and enter the province to the south. We crossed over the Restigouche River, remorseful that we were leaving our French friends but looking forward to visiting the Maritimes.

Dozens of travelers had told us they especially enjoyed this part of Canada. We were about to find out why.

7

NEW BRUNSWICK

"Vive l' Acadie!"

Credo noted on Acadian artifacts

The receptionist at the tourist-information building in Campbell town reminded us to set our watches ahead since Quebec is on Eastern time while New Brunswick (as well as Prince Edward Island and Nova Scotia) is an hour ahead on Atlantic time.

Newfoundland is another half-hour ahead of these Maritime Provinces. A half-hour, not an hour. We were told Newfies enjoy having their own unique time zone.

After picking up a provincial map and several tourist brochures, we headed south to a campground near Miramichi. Highway 11 is a well-traveled two-lane highway reminiscent of northern Ontario with bush on both sides and occasional MOOSE signs.

To be closer to the water, we diverted to Acadian Coastal Drive and passed through several seaside villages, which were distinctly different from those in Gaspé. Most noticeably, all the houses were painted white. According to a local artist, "White paint is cheaper than coloured. Only newer houses with aluminum siding tend to be coloured." Industry was disturbingly intrusive, including a lumber mill, peat-moss plant, and power-generating facility. And most distressing, the road was extremely rough, slowing our pace to a snail's crawl. At first opportunity, we returned to the main highway and proceeded to our campground.

The next day we walked Elly to a nearby historical site, consisting of a rebuilt church, cemetery, and memorial. This was our first exposure to the struggles of Acadians during the 1700's. While Elly lolled in the shade of an oak tree, a tour guide explained the early history of Acadians in Eastern Canada.

"Acadia" was the name given to the three Maritime Provinces, occupied by French pioneers who sought a peaceful life of farming and fishing. After the British conquered these lands, the Acadians were required to swear an oath to the King of England, which meant they would have to take up arms against the French. Most refused.

Consequently, in 1755, Britain deported over 6000 resident Acadians to France, England, and various American colonies, including Louisiana where today, their descendants are known as "Cajuns." About ten years later, the deportees were allowed to return.

Since their previous homesteads had been taken over by New England farmers, many moved to desolate locations where they could start anew. The church and cemetery were remnants of one such settlement, and the DEPORTATION MEMORIAL testifies to their sacrifices. Through faith, persistence, and hard work, the Arcadians managed to maintain their culture, evident in many Maritime communities we would visit.

The Acadian flag—red, white, and blue horizontal stripes with a distinctive yellow star—flew proudly throughout New Brunswick and Nova Scotia. These colors and the star were applied in creative ways to just about everything: fence posts, benches, lawn ornaments, barns, lobster traps, and even the telephone poles in Cape Pelé, reportedly the geographical centre of the Maritimes. In support of these remarkable Canadians, we purchased an Acadian flag and flew it proudly from the truck antenna for the remainder of our journey.

Due to their infusion into primarily English-speaking provinces, most Acadians we met were bilingual. One man related an interesting story of an event that occurred during the deportation. The British had rounded up all the Acadian men and women of a small village and separated them by sex, putting all males on one ship and all females on another. Their intent was to destroy the Acadian culture by taking them to different locations. Unbeknownst to them, a man by the surname of Cormier had dressed as a woman, permitting him and his wife to live together and procreate in their new settlement. As a result, a large number of Acadians, including the storyteller, have retained that name today.

This same middle-aged gentleman expressed envy at our lifestyle and wanted to do the same when he retired in another "6 years, 4 months, and 23 days." I suspect he disliked his job! He sheepishly asked, "How much does it cost to do what you're doing, living on the road rather than in a house?"

"Well, it costs pretty much the same," I replied, " but it's a heck of a lot more fun." Certainly, the major expenses of full-time RVing—fuel, campground fees, and activity fees—can be controlled to fit almost any budget. Some studies have shown that RVers can live comfortably on less than $2000 per month. Those who travel more, stay at fancier resorts, and participate in more activities such as golf, dining out, and sightseeing will likely spend more. Spending less might mean more dry camping or staying in no-frills campgrounds, of which there are many. I suspect that most full-timers will match their lifestyle to their budget, much as we were doing during our cross-country trip: our expenses closely matched what we were spending as homeowners in Powell River.

When you're on a perpetual holiday, you tend to lose track of the days. My pillbox told me it was Wednesday.

The day started like most but turned out to be the most stressful of our trip. After a leisurely breakfast, we packed up and headed south toward our next campground at Cap Lumiére (Cape Light). Acadian Coastal Drive was bumpy from the get go, holding us to speeds under 50 kph. Elly coped by bracing herself with one foot on the floor hump. Simone slept soundly in her cage while Buster bounced gently on his bed between our front seats. We fully expected him to upchuck, but he didn't, even after a half-hour of bouncing. In fact, he didn't upchuck for the remainder of our trip, even on the roughest roads. I can only assume that prolonged exposure to the bumpy roads of New Brunswick acted to relax Buster, much like the prolonged curvy road in British Columbia. Regardless of the reason, we were happy that our little guy was no longer stressed by either curvy or bumpy roads. That was the good news for the day.

Along the way, we passed through Kouchibouguac National Park, stopping at the Park Information Centre to inquire, for future reference, whether they could accommodate a rig of our size. They said they could, but we had already reserved for that evening at a private campground.

When parking, I would typically lower the front and back power windows in the truck a few centimetres to provide air for the critters. I did so in this instance since we planned to spend about 15 minutes in the Centre.

Upon returning, we noticed that Buster was missing. He had apparently gotten up on Simone's cage and jumped out the rear window, which I had inadvertently left open more than usual.

We immediately checked the parking lot area; then asked a few picnickers if they had seen a big grey cat with a red collar. One couple had seen him "just five minutes ago entering a culvert at the entrance to the parking lot."

Unfortunately, by the time we got there, he was no longer in the culvert. But at least we had a starting point.

After an hour of frantic searching, I suggested to Sandy that she post a LOST CAT notice on the Centre door with Buster's picture, which we carried for just such emergencies. I then got Elly out of the truck to help search, but she wasn't much of a tracking dog: *Perhaps if I had been trained to track, I could find Buster. In the meantime, I'll just sniff whatever comes along and enjoy my walk in the woods.*

That dog can be a little self-centred at times.

Sandy and I had already discussed camping in the parking lot for as long as it took to find Buster. A veterinarian had once told us that 80% of cats that run away find their way back home, eventually. While that might be true in a familiar residential neighbourhood, I would think the odds are considerably lower for a cat that runs away from a trailer in the middle of a National Park.

While Sandy was preparing the note, I kept searching, trying to think like an old cat. Where would I go if I were Buster? The busy road would be scary. On the other hand, the dense underbrush in the woods would be difficult.

I decided the grassy ditch beside the less-traveled road away from the parking lot would be his route of choice and continued walking along it, pausing occasionally to peer into the woods and holler "Buster!" About 100 metres along, I looked ahead and sure enough, there he was, just strolling along the shoulder of an intersecting dirt road. As I ran toward him, he scurried into the woods, obviously intent on avoiding capture. For a brief panic-stricken minute, he was lost again. "Buster!"

Charging out of the underbrush like a cheetah on steroids, he ran across the road, down into a ditch, through a culvert, and back toward the parking lot. Nearing the lot, he suddenly stopped to catch his breath. I was never so happy to gather him up in my arms as I was at that moment.

Sandy was also overjoyed to see that Buster was safely back home.

Elly commented, what great fun, we should do that more often!

And Simone slept through it all.

After more corrugated roads, highway construction forced us to detour ten kilometres out of our way. Reaching our campground, we discovered that one living-room drawer had completely distributed its contents on the floor, another had broken loose from its plastic slides, a ceiling light was hanging from its wires, and a couple of screws had broken on the rear ladder that carried our bicycles.

A camper earlier in our trip, when I mentioned the rough roads in Quebec, offered his opinion: "New Brunswick has even rougher roads, the worst in Canada."

Although main highways were reasonably smooth, secondary roads definitely needed resurfacing. Perhaps they might have felt smoother in a car, but towing a heavy trailer with a truck added a whole new dimension of "cringing" to our travels.

What a day! Life had gone from horribly frightful to joyously delightful in just a few hours. Good thing I can think like an old cat.

Lounging and sipping Titantics at our grassy campsite beside a salt-shaker lighthouse, we gazed out across the tranquil Northumberland Strait. On the distant horizon, the low profile of Prince Edward Island was hatched by the lights of Confederation Bridge, sparkling like stars in a darkening sky.

Most of the night, Buster raced back and forth between our bed and the rear window as if on a primal chase in the wilderness. Fortunately, by the next night he was back to his old self, sleeping contentedly curled up in our bed.

We camped for a couple of days near Shediac, the "Lobster Capital of the World." Here Elly nonchalantly met the "World's Largest Lobster," standing five metres high and weighing 90 tons.

What is it?

"It's a lobster and lives on the bottom of the sea," I replied.

OK...oh look, there's a squirrel!

This fibreglass sculpture was painted in shades of brown and yellow, simulating their natural colour. Except for the rare albino lobster, which is naturally red, lobsters only turn red after cooking.

Lobster sculpture in Shediac, New Brunswick

I intended to have a lobster dinner in Shediac, but our camping neighbour told me to try the fried clams at a local eatery, "the best ever, if you like clams." I thought I did, especially steamed clams dipped in drawn butter, which were served at local festivals during my youth in Pennsylvania. But these, piled high on a paper plate, were fried in batter, greasy and tough. After chewing each clam, I felt prudent to remove a piece of something the size and consistency of a Number Two pencil eraser. To this day, I still wonder what that body part was and whether my camping neighbour actually swallowed it.

Nearby Cape-Pelé is a small colourful fishing village known as the "Smokehouse Capital of Canada." Its several dozen smokehouses provide about 95 percent of Canada's smoked herring, much of it exported to other countries through the port of Halifax. Although some smokehouses offer tours, all were closed for July and August because they were too hot inside for the employees.

At a local gallery, many of the paintings showed clotheslines with wash swinging in the breeze, a scene we had first noticed in the Gaspé region and would continue to see throughout the Maritimes. I didn't recall seeing similar paintings in western Canada.

An Acadian woman explained why clotheslines are so prevalent: "It's cheaper to hang up wash than to use a dryer; clothes dry quickly in the wind and sunshine." She continued, "Once, I hung out three pairs of my husband's long johns and noticed that tourists were stopping to take photos!"

Apparently, the display of laundry strikes a cord with the artistically inclined. Being of similar ilk, Sandy bought several small paintings displaying laundry in the foreground.

Later that evening, we attended the finale of a local talent show, one that had been occurring over several weeks. The contestants were three young female singers. Each sang three songs—two in French, one in English—after which the audience rated their performance. All had powerful voices, but Sandy and I both agreed on the eventual winner, who is surely destined for stardom.

After a morning stroll along Parlee Beach near our campground, we drove across Confederation Bridge to Prince Edward Island. Since we would visit more of New Brunswick on our return trip, I maintained the authenticity of our travels by including that portion in a later chapter.

Larry MacDonald, Ph.D.

8

PRINCE EDWARD ISLAND

"The Birthplace of Canada"

Quote from a tour guide

Confederation Bridge is an ultramodern structure, 13 kilometres in length, reportedly the longest freestanding bridge in the world over freezing water. The water freezes here because salt water from the Atlantic Ocean is diluted by fresh water from the St. Lawrence and other rivers that flow into the Gulf. While most of its length is low near the water, the centre arches like a whale's backbone high above the Northumberland Strait. At the summit, Sandy described a breathtaking vista of green hills, red cliffs, seaside villages, and a sparkling blue sea far below. I dared not look.

Immediately after crossing, we stopped at Gateway Village, a 1900-vintage streetscape that includes restaurants, retail outlets, and the all-important Visitor Centre. The agent informed us that the island is divided into three regions for tourism purposes—east, central, and west—each having a scenic drive. We picked up a supply of brochures and a map on which the agent had drawn an orange line showing the best route to our campground near Charlottetown.

The Trans-Canada Highway (properly designated Route 1) meandered through a landscape reminiscent of a pop-up storybook, orderly and well defined. Extensive green fields of potato plants alternated with yellow fields of wheat and barley; homes with gabled windows and cozy verandas were surrounded by lawns the size of football fields, neatly manicured and landscaped with wild flowers. Even the clear blue sky was replete with puffy white clouds. Following the practice of her mom, Sandy pointed out one that resembled a jellyfish with a crown of white, trailing wisps below. Elly kept her eyes peeled for cows.

While I was setting up camp, Sandy and Elly were playing a routine game of hide-and-seek. Sandy would hide behind a tree and yell, "FIND ME!" which signaled Elly to run happily in the direction of her voice. Unfortunately, on this occasion she stepped in a gopher hole, whimpered, and came up limping. *I'm OK, I'm OK. Just give me a minute and I'll be ready to play again.*

Her leg wasn't broken, but she walked gingerly for a few days and had to be carried in and out of the trailer. Our vet says that dogs don't feel pain the same way humans do. How can she know that? When I sprain my leg, I whimper, limp, and walk gingerly for a few days although Sandy refuses to carry me in and out of the trailer! Maybe I play the sympathy card a bit longer than Elly, but that's the only difference I can detect.

Prince Edward Island, PEI, is considered the birthplace of Canada. In 1864, a meeting of politicians was held in Charlottetown, the capital city. Their intent was to discuss the unification of the three Maritime Provinces: New Brunswick, Nova Scotia, and Prince Edward Island. However, representatives from Ontario and Quebec (then known as Upper and Lower Canada) arrived to discuss a wider union of provinces, from sea to sea, for political, economic, and military benefits.

After a week of daytime discussions and evening parties, the delegates agreed to meet a month later in Quebec City to draft a constitution of this new nation. John A. MacDonald, the delegate from Ontario, became Canada's first Prime Minister after Britain agreed to the terms of Confederation. Ontario, Quebec, Nova Scotia, and New Brunswick were the first to join Confederation on July 1, 1867, followed a few years later by Manitoba and British Columbia.

Unlike the United States, which proclaimed its independence from Britain, Canada became a Commonwealth Country under the authority of the British Empire and remains so today. Most Canadians seem to prefer this arrangement, as was evident at the recent Canada Day celebrations in Ottawa where Queen Elizabeth was given a royal welcome by multitudes of well wishers.

Interestingly, PEI chose not to join Confederation in 1867. Skeptical island folks were not convinced they would benefit since their shipbuilding, farming, and fishing enterprises were all prospering. Why would they even consider paying federal taxes? Six years later, however, a burdening financial debt prompted them to join when Canada agreed to assume the debt.

Newfoundland held out even longer, taking pride in being a sovereign state for nearly a hundred years. Following WWII, in 1949 their tenuous financial situation, and desire to be part of a larger community were arguments in favour of joining Canada.

We learned more about these historic events during a walking tour of Charlottetown, guided by a knowledgeable young lady in period costume. Along the way to Province House where the original meetings occurred, we encountered several more costumed actors, including the town crier, a tavern sweeper, and "John A. MacDonald" himself. It was great fun and very informative, as was the Founder's Hall museum, which provides interactive exhibits using popular TV personalities to describe these eventful times.

Province House, PEI with costumed actors

PEI is well known for its red sandstone cliffs, red sand beaches, and red dirt roads. But, for most Canadians, the mention of PEI conjures up images of a spunky, red headed orphan girl that Lucy Maude Montgomery immortalized in her 1908 book, *Anne of Green Gables*. Carefully cultivated fields, peaceful forests, flowered meadows, and gentle ocean waves lapping fine sand beaches inspired Montgomery to write about her homeland.

Over 100 years later, it's still all here in Cavendish on the North Shore just as the famous author described. And hopefully, it will remain so, due in no small measure to the efforts of the LM Montgomery Land Trust, a nonprofit organization dedicated to preserving these cherished lands for future generations. It behooves the province to do so since a major tourist industry—museums, stores, theatrical productions, an entire village, and endless memorabilia—has developed around the character of Anne, attracting people from all over the world.

The play, *Anne of Green Gables,* which had been running continuously for 46 years, is a rollicking musical with a message of hope. We left the theatre feeling joyful as well as a bit hungry so we sought out one of many popular sidewalk cafes scattered about downtown Charlottetown.

Near our table, a slew of young folks dressed to the nines, postured unabashedly, as a jazz band played in the background. Much like Ottawa, there was no evidence of a national recession in this community.

After a few days exploring the Charlottetown area, we relocated a short distance to Brudenell River Provincial Park on the eastern shore. Whenever we visited a community, we highlighted our route with a felt-tip pen. Within a few days, the eastern portion of our map looked like a spider web with strands reaching out in all directions from our campsite.

Our first trip was to a lighthouse at the eastern-most point, appropriately called East Point. Along the way, we spoke to two lobster fishermen at Launching Point, a working harbour complete with rows of aging boats bobbing at wooden docks. Both men had fished for nearly 50 years. When we inquired about the lobster season which had just ended, both agreed they were happy with the number and size of their catch but disappointed with the selling price: about $3.00 per pound. Knowing that consumers were paying $20 in local restaurants and $100 in Japan for a one-pound lobster, the more talkative man, writhing his callused hands, lamented: "Lobster fishermen are a dying breed. The season is only two months so we need to do something else to earn a living. Cod fishing is not an option. We outsmarted ourselves by over-fishing when cod were plentiful; now we're paying the price." Sadly, even if they wanted to get out of the business, there were no buyers for their traps or their boats, which sat idle most of the year.

I suggested that they consider forming a "Lobster Pool" similar to a Wheat Pool, which sets commodity prices. They didn't think it would work because their buyers would say, "take it or leave it" when they offered $3.00 per pound.

"But," I retorted, somewhat out of my depth, "if all the lobster fishermen in PEI refused to sell unless they were paid a fair price, say five dollars a pound as determined by the Pool, then the buyers wouldn't be able to purchase lobster."

The man seemed to follow my logic but quickly replied with frustration in his voice, "ahh...buyers would just go elsewhere, like Nova Scotia, to get their lobster."

I didn't pursue the notion of a "Maritime Lobster Pool." Instead, we wished them well and walked back to the truck past stacks of lobster traps that would soon be stored in dockside sheds, protected from winter winds as frigid as these fishermen's spirits.

Farther up coast, we visited the renowned "Singing Sands Beach" near Basin Head where, according to our brochure, the sand actually sings when the wind blows. During our visit, the wind wasn't blowing hard enough to promote singing, but the sand did make low-pitched squeaks when we dragged our feet across the surface. The beach was crowded, as was a wooded bridge from which youngsters were jumping into a salt-water tributary to the delight of their friends and onlookers. Fortunately, I hadn't brought my swimsuit!

After visiting East Point Lighthouse, we continued along the north shore to Hermanville, site of the only distillery in Canada that makes potato vodka. The brewer said it takes 30 pounds of potatoes to make one bottle of vodka. The sample I tried definitely tasted like taters, but their wild-blueberry gin brought a twinkle to my eye. We bought two bottles for special occasions, which seemed to be rather frequent during our travels.

On a particularly fine day, we visited historic Georgetown, a short drive eastward. According to a poster board, one-third of the buildings were constructed before or during the 1920's. The architecture looked very British with low gable and dormer windows projecting from steep roofs.

The library was a two-room affair: one contained books; the other computers, which we used to check our email. It was the smallest library imaginable, about the size of the trailer, giving us the feeling that we had been captured in a 100-year time warp. Later, at a popular seafood restaurant, the menu offered a tip for buying fish: "If it smells like the ocean, it's nice. If it smells like fish, think twice." Their seafood chow-da was the best I had tasted on the Island.

The following day, we drove along the south shore to Woods Island, where a ferry operates to and from Nova Scotia. Along the way, we stopped at Cape Bear to visit an historic lighthouse, one of seven on the island that still operates today. A Marconi Wireless Station, manned here in the early 1900's, was reportedly the first Canadian station to receive an SOS distress signal from a sinking Titanic off the coast of Newfoundland. When I asked our guide why that same signal wasn't received in Newfoundland, she smiled and said, "It may have been, but they were not part of Canada at the time. They only joined confederation in 1949."

Farther south along the coast, we came across a boutique in Murray Harbour called "Miss Elly's." Fortunately, our Miss Elly was with us so we stopped to get a photo of her on the front porch.

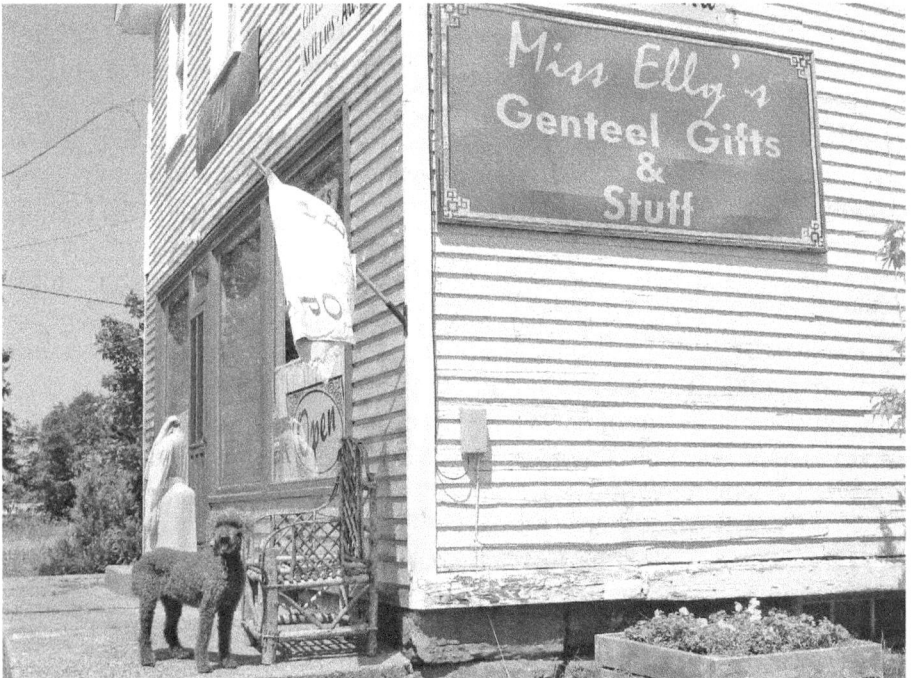

Miss Elly at Miss Elly's, Murray Harbour, PEI

Earlier in our trip in northern Ontario, we stopped for lunch at "Busters." Now all we needed to do was find an establishment called "Simone's"— a true "hat trick." That expression, by the way, refers to a hockey player making three goals in a game, or in this case, three similar events. The name originated in the 1940's when a Toronto businessman offered a free hat to any Maple Leaf player scoring three goals in one game. We learned this trivial tidbit in Montreal when visiting the fur-trading museum. I can hardly wait until someone asks, "Where do you suppose the name 'hat trick' came from?"

PEI is Canada's smallest Province: we could drive its width in half an hour, from tip to tip in less than four hours, being never more than 17 kilometres from salt water. The railroad system that had branched across the island in the early 1900's proved to be not only expensive to build and operate, but unnecessary. Transport trucks became more efficient in transporting goods. Consequently, the tracks were removed and the abandoned railway lines became Confederation Trail, popular today with bicyclists and hikers. We decided to bike on what was billed "the most scenic section of Confederation Trail" between the villages of Morell and St. Peters. Renting our bikes in Morell, we peddled unhurriedly through woods and pastures, following a flat gravel path that meandered along the south shore of St. Peters Bay. Several old wooden bridges complemented the pastoral ambience.

The long narrow bay was dotted with rows of buoyed ropes used to cultivate blue mussels. "Many consider them the best tasting mussels in the world. If you like mussels, you'll love PEI mussels," is how a fellow biker spoke about her plate of mussels as we dined on the patio of a popular eatery in St. Peters.

After lunch, we backtracked to Morell for an ice cream dessert. Along the way, we chatted briefly with other bikers, some intending to peddle the entire 270 kilometres of Confederation Trail. Campsites, B&B's, and hostels are plentiful along the trail. Everyone we met said "Hello," "Bonjour," or gave a friendly wave. Another happy and memorable day!

Leaving the east region of PEI, we followed one of our strands back to Charlottetown, where we dry camped in a shopping centre. The next morning, we headed north to a campground near Darnley, following Central Coastal Drive. "WOW!" This section of roadway was one of the prettiest we had seen during our travels, anywhere. The rugged coastline and picturesque fishing villages, such as French River, had us stopping frequently to absorb the scenery and take photos.

Pastoral scene along Central Coastal Drive, PEI

During the next five days, I played a couple rounds of golf near Cavendish while Sandy perused craft shops and art galleries. Elly mostly pet-sat her brother and sister. One morning as I was putting on my golf shoes, she stood in front of me and stared into my eyes, deeply, trying to get a sense of whether she was going with me. *Am I going with you? Am I? Am I please?*

"Not today Elly. We'll go for a walk later, okay?"

Of course, we both knew it wasn't okay. Sometimes, for a minute or so after we closed the door she'd howl, making a soulful sound that no parent could ignore. On those occasions, we pretended she was someone else's dog.

But upon our return, Elly would always welcome us with delightful squeaks and wiggles. *Can we go for a walk now? Can we? Like you promised?*

"Okay, let's get your collar on."

Off we'd go to the nearest patch of green where she'd do her business and sniff about where other dogs had tread. Then, we'd walk down a trail or around the campground where people would typically ask, "What kind of dog is that?" "A Standard Poodle," I'd reply. More often than not, they'd say, "He's small for a poodle," after which I would advise them, "Well, she's pretty much average size for a female." I always wanted to add that her Dad was a champion and she could have been also … had it not been for her bad breath!

Summerside, PEI's second largest city of 16,000 people, is situated at the gateway to the province's western region. Our pre-booked ferry to Newfoundland, August 18, did not allow time for us to visit this region. However, we did spend a day browsing Summerside's waterfront, its boardwalk and several gift shops and art galleries each brightly coloured green, blue, red, and yellow. Four city-owned wind turbines turned briskly nearby. Based on my earlier knowledge gleaned in Quebec, each turbine produces enough electricity for 4000 homes, significantly reducing the need for more polluting sources of energy. We were pleasantly surprised that conservation is so popular here: in addition to wind turbines, recycling boxes are common in campgrounds and even on downtown sidewalks, supporting PEI's reputation as the Green Island.

Nearing the end of our allotted two weeks, we lamented that our planning could have been better. Firstly, we should have allocated a week to explore the west region. Secondly, we were so excited about visiting PEI we never gave much thought about leaving. We should have. The ferry to Nova Scotia leaves from the eastern region, which we had visited earlier. Now, when it was time to leave, we found ourselves in the central region near Confederation Bridge. So, we took it. Visitors do not pay to enter, either by bridge or by ferry. They do, however, pay to leave. Although the bridge is less expensive than the ferry, the cost of driving the additional distance through New Brunswick to Nova Scotia, in our case, would have more than covered the additional ferry fee. Andy was programmed to take the shorter route so he kept telling us, "Make a U-Turn," even in the middle of the bridge. We finally put him on "Mute" and continued the long way around to Nova Scotia.

Larry MacDonald, Ph.D.

9

NOVA SCOTIA

"Don't forget your camera"

Comment of tourist agent

We crossed the border near Amherst and, you guessed it, stopped at the Travel Information Centre for maps and brochures. Highway 6 took us through rolling hills and small communities along the Northumberland Shore. Within a couple of hours, we passed through Pictou near where the ferry from PEI would have dropped us off. The word "hindsight" came to mind. Andy was just dying to say in his calm and robotic voice: "I told you so."

That evening, we camped at a shopping centre in New Glasgow. While Sandy was talking on the phone to a friend in Ontario, she suddenly shrieked and shouted, "I just saw a mouse!" I had also seen it, running across the carpet and behind the couch, although Elly and the normally watchful felines did not. Exactly how it got in was not clear, nor did it matter. The more important question was: how would it get out?

In the middle of the night, we were awakened by the sounds of a skirmish in the kitchen. Buster had apparently encountered the visitor and was freewheeling on the linoleum floor as if on ice skates. Failing in his pursuit, he eventually came to bed. However, the next morning while tethered outside, he captured a mouse that looked identical to the one we had seen. I disposed of it and we never again saw a mouse inside. We assumed the unfortunate little guy had left the same way he got in, at the most inopportune time. Only Buster knew for sure, and he wasn't talking.

The next day, we continued east to Cape Breton, which I had always pictured as a peninsula in northeastern Nova Scotia. Well, it is and it isn't! Cape Breton is an island connected to the rest of the province by a man-made causeway across the Strait of Canso. Its well known feature is indeed a peninsula fringed by the 300 km Cabot Trail. Camping at Baddeck for five days afforded the opportunity to explore the Trail as well as the surrounding area. Sections of this two-lane road snake steeply upwards toward heavily treed highlands, then downwards toward the sea, never far from the rugged coastline. *Lonely Planet* calls it "one of the world's best road trips." Along the way, Elly heard lots of "Ohs" and "Ahs," but seldom looked out the window, figuring there were no cows about. Strategically placed pullouts called LOOK OFFS allow breathtaking views of distant headlands, fishing villages, and endless seascapes. Moose and whale sightings are common, although we saw neither.

While trucking up the eastern side from Baddeck, Sandy expressed her feelings about being on the outside edge as somewhere between thrill and terror. She called it "tingle." Although the road is wide enough to accommodate large buses, some sections required total concentration: even a slight distraction might have turned the truck into an airplane, albeit briefly. Road signs printed in Gaelic and English and a Gaelic college reflect the strong Scottish influence in this area.

We drove through Cape Breton Highland National Park, then further north along a gravel road to Meat Cove, a small community perched on a scenic headland. While dining on the patio of a small café with an unobstructed view of Nirvana, I asked our waitress about the town's name. She said that early sailing ships used to stop here to replenish their supply of moose meat.

"Well then," I quipped, "shouldn't it be called Moose Meat Cove?" She just smiled and rolled her eyes, probably hoping we'd leave soon.

Many tourists travel the entire loop in one day, four hours without stopping, but we chose to go back down the eastern side. Not only would it give us a different perspective, it would provide an opportunity to visit a quaint fishing village we by-passed on the way up, Neil's Harbour, as well as the pink granite boulders we had read about in a brochure. We were pleased to see that the mountains were covered in dense evergreens, unlike BC with its wretched patches of clear-cut and pine-beetle infestations.

The next day, we drove up the western side of the peninsula to Pleasant Bay, where the Trail leaves the coast and turns eastward across the top of the National Park. Along the way, we stopped at Cap le Moine to see a display of Joe's Scarecrows. It all started in 1984 when Joe planted a garden and set up three fully-dressed scarecrows to keep animals away. Tourists stopped to take photos, so he added more, and more, until his field of nearly 100 scarecrows became a popular tourist site, attracting thousands of visitors each year. Some have faces of famous celebrities such as Brian Mulroney, Bill Clinton, and Margaret Thatcher; others depict everyday working folks. A group of children scarecrows were playing "Ring Around the Rosie" with a space for any child who wanted to join in and have their photo taken. Great family entertainment!

Author amidst Joe's Scarecrows at Cap le Moine, Cape Breton, Nova Scotia

In the community of Cheticamp, we visited an Acadian church and later dined on the outside patio of Wabo Pizza House. According to their menu, the word "Wabo" means "a time of rejoicing, sharing, good spirits, and brotherhood." Our waitress estimated that 80 percent of the town folks are Acadian, speaking both French and English. Sandy practiced her French with nearby patrons, even though they spoke fluent English. At the church, an Acadian flag flew at the entrance, and across the water on a small island was another, waving on a pole stuck in the rocks. These symbols of patriotism made us proud of a group of French Canadians who struggled to maintain their culture through centuries of hardships.

Alexander Graham Bell is best known as the inventor of the telephone. Although Canada sometimes takes credit for the invention, the story is a bit more complicated. Born in Scotland in 1847, Bell came to Canada with his family at age 23, residing near Brantford, Ontario where he conceived the idea of talking through wires. He later moved to Washington, D.C. where at age 29 he put his ideas into practice with the famous words, "Mr. Watson; come here; I want to see you." Bell considered himself American even though the last 37 years of his life were spent in Baddeck. Here, he continued to apply his creative genius to other endeavours, including the first powered airplane flight in Canada and a hydrofoil boat, the fastest in the world at the time. A museum in Baddeck provides a treasure trove of audio-visual exhibits, photographs, and artifacts detailing the life of this remarkable man.

Our museum tour guide mentioned some additional tidbits about Bell's personal life. In his mid-twenties as a teacher of deaf youngsters, he fell in love with one of his students, Mabel, who was just 16 at the time. With her parent's permission, they married when she turned 18. Her wealthy father provided funding for Bell's research on the telephone.

When Bell successfully received a patent, he gave nearly all of his Bell Telephone stock to his wife, making her a very wealthy woman. They bought 500 acres of land on a peninsula jutting out into Bras d'Or Lake (pronounced Bra-Door Lake) and built a huge mansion with a laboratory where Bell spent much of his time inventing. According to Bell, "An inventor can no more help inventing than he can help thinking or breathing." I feel the same way about a traveler. Bell would often spend late night hours in his laboratory, working on some obscure project. His wife, an artist, painted a portrait of him, which he wasn't allowed to see until it was finished. When that day arrived, she summoned him to her studio and removed the drape from the canvas—displaying an owl.

We were still in Baddeck on my birthday, August 16, so Sandy treated me to a round of golf at a local course overlooking the lake. I didn't need an excuse to play golf, but sunny weather and the well-groomed course beckoned. Later, we took a harbour cruise on a 70-foot sailboat, the Amoeba, from which we could see Bell's magnificent mansion and nearby houses on land still owned and occupied by his descendants. The Captain pointed out the house of one of Bell's daughters who married the founder of the National Geographic Society.

A bald eagle circled the boat, prompting the Captain to throw a frozen fish overboard. As soon as it hit the water, the eagle dove with claws extended, snatching it up and flying off to a distant tree to enjoy the meal. This cruise happens three times a day, giving the eagle lots of opportunities to teach the Captain to throw food its way. As the cruise was ending, the Captain whispered to us that one of Bell's great grandchildren happened to be on board but preferred not to be identified. He then surreptitiously pointed out the elderly gentleman. I thought briefly about requesting an interview, but Sandy squelched that idea in no uncertain terms.

That evening, we dined at the Silver Dart Restaurant, named after the airplane that made the first powered flight in Canada, six years after the Wright brothers, in February 1909. I don't mind getting older when birthdays are that memorable.

After doing laundry at the campground, we packed up and drove southeast to Sydney where we stayed overnight in a shopping centre. Our ferry to Newfoundland, which we had booked two months earlier, was scheduled to leave North Sydney at 10 am the next day. We had been advised to arrive at least an hour and a half before departure. True to form we were late, so late that we were the last vehicle to board. Sunny skies and calm seas provided perfect conditions for a sea-going voyage. During the six-hour crossing, pets are not allowed topside, nor were we allowed to go down to our vehicle. Elly and Buster, who had ridden BC ferries dozens of times, likely slept most of the way. We hoped, perhaps in vain, that Simone did likewise.

Standing on the upper deck while getting underway took me back to my Navy days. Whenever our ship left harbour, I got goose bumps, excited to be going someplace new, perhaps even to a foreign land. That same feeling pervaded me as the dock lines were cast off and we maneuvered out to open water. This very modern ferry was outfitted with private cabins, a spa, Wifi, bar, and several restaurants. We settled into some comfortable chairs and spent time checking email, reading, and listening to a guitar player who took requests. I asked her if she knew Kenny Roger's "The Gambler." She did, and to my delight many of the passengers sang along, "You never count your money, when you're sittin' at the table ...."

Larry MacDonald, Ph.D.

10

NEWFOUNDLAND

"She's gone boy, she's gone."

A cod fisherman's comment about the good old days

The excitement returned as a loudspeaker announced our arrival at Channel-Port-aux-Basque on the southwest corner of Newfoundland. From topside, we watched the huge ship maneuver through a narrow channel, turning completely around so that vehicles could drive out the stern gangway. We managed to be one of the first off, which allowed us to beat the crowds to the Travel Information Centre. A fellow camper from Newfoundland had forewarned us: "Newfies are a different breed," he said jovially, "They'll talk your arse off."

Sure enough, the gal behind the counter kept chatting with us and circling places on the map that we "must see" during our visit, seemingly oblivious to the increasing long line up of eager tourists seeking her attention. Throughout our stay, we noted repeatedly that Newfies seem to enjoy a "good chin-wag."

The Trans-Canada Highway runs from Channel-Port-aux-Basques halfway up the west coast to Deer Lake, then arcs 600 kilometres across the province to St. John's on the southeast coast. At Deer Lake, the Viking Trail (Route 430) follows the coastline to the tip of the Northern Peninsula, as far as one can drive. We planned to explore the west coast for a couple of weeks before heading east.

Driving north from the ferry terminal, the landscape was dramatically different from anything we had ever seen, rocky and barren with small water-filled craters and sparse vegetation. "Like being on the surface of the moon" was how our friend Ian had described it.

We were repeatedly reminded why the locals refer to this island as "The Rock." One Newfie said it's because, "Newfoundland anchors the rest of Canada." Based on our limited assessment, it definitely vies for top spot with Bobcaygeon as "the rockiest place on the planet."

Less than an hour's drive north near Codroy Valley, we stopped at a campground for the night. Friends had told us about the splendour of this lush valley so we wanted to spend some time here, but decided to do so on our way back to the ferry. The Newfies in the campground office, the only location we could receive Wifi, were so effusive that Sandy never did get to her email. Sandy would be the first to admit she enjoys conversing with complete strangers. Me, not so much. After an exchange of pleasantries, I'll mumble something about needing to check my email. End of discussion. However, my ears perked up when a local described a nearby area called "Wreckhouse," where 200 kph winds sometimes funnel down steep passes in the Long Range Mountains. "Even fully loaded semis are overturned in the blink of an eye. You don't want to be on the road when the semis are parked." Later in our travels, I spoke to a camper who had actually seen an overturned semi caused by the previous day's winds in Wreckhouse.

The next morning, I was eager to get out on the highway to see if the semis were parked. They weren't. We passed through a becalmed Wreckhouse without incident. As a cruising sailor with a journalistic bent, I often wrote about various destinations, hoping that some catastrophic event would occur to spice up my story, such as colliding with a whale or being boarded by pirates. Today, I was hoping the semis were parked!

We continued to a campground near Stephensville (pronounced Stevensville), a small town with the stark appearance of an abandoned military base. We found out later it was exactly that. During WWII, the United States built a base here that was used to train pilots and store provisions. After the war, the unneeded Quonset-shaped buildings were donated to the town, where some continue to be used in commerce.

Unhitching the trailer, we drove west along the French Ancestor's Route on the Port au Port Peninsula, a triangle of land that juts out into the Gulf of St. Lawrence. Our first stop was Sheaves Cove where shoreline rocks have unique formations, layered, some resembling caskets. Elly commented excitedly, *Look over there — that one looks like a cat.*

I can just hear her telling her canine friends: *On a rocky beach, there's no reason to be bored.*

Continuing on to Cape St. George, we parked next to a French-built replica of a 19th Century bread oven, made of bricks and mortar. Although it wasn't being used, we could almost smell the enticing odor of freshly baking Baguettes.

A short looping path called Bread Crumb Trail took us through wind-tortured evergreens, known locally as Tuckamores. We saw many such stunted, shredded trees along the west coast, their gnarled and twisted bark evidence of fierce onshore winds that sweep across the Gulf of St. Lawrence.

At the extreme end of the peninsula, an interesting rock formation resembled a boot about the size of our ferry upended. Residents of the cape include a colony of Northern Gannets. We watched in fascination as several of these large white seabirds with distinctive black wingtips soared gracefully high above the water in search of herring or mackerel.

Selecting their prey, they folded their wings, two metres from tip to tip, and dove straight down, hitting the water with a spectacular splash. Within seconds, they were again airborne, seeking altitude in search of another morsel.

The encroaching darkness prevented further exploration of this penin-sula so we backtracked through villages along the coastline. People waved enthusiastically from their porches, making us feel as welcomed as kinfolk. We waved back, a re-occurring scenerio throughout this province. While Canadians in general are friendly, we found those in Newfoundland to be definitely the most expressive. We liked it here.

Occasionally with friends, Sandy and I will initiate a game where each person is asked to select eight individuals that they would invite to dinner. The invitees can be anyone, dead or alive, perhaps Michelangelo, Christ, Mandela, Lennon, or whomever. It's fun to find out why a particular person was chosen. Steinbeck would be one of my invitees—provided he brought Charley. That way, Elly would get a chance to meet her counterpart, per-haps off in a corner somewhere, while John and I compared countries.

Another of my invitees, because of my interest in sailing and exploring, would be Captain James Cook, best known for his exploits in the South Pa-cific. I'd had the opportunity to visit Cook's boyhood home in England, his gravesite in Hawaii, and to sail the same coastal waters in British Colum-bia as he did on HMS Resolution. However, I knew little about his earlier years: commanding a British ship in Canadian waters during the French and English seven-year war (1756 63) and charting the coastline of New-foundland over a subsequent five-year period.

A monument near the town of Corner Brook provided this information and more. Reportedly, Cook's charts were so detailed that they could still be used today to navigate these treacherous waters. Because of his surveying skills and competence as a sailor and astronomer, the Royal Society selected him to explore the unknown reaches of the South Pacific.

Elly at Captain James Cook Historic Site in Corner Brook, Newfoundland

At Corner Brook, we dry camped in a shopping centre while we explored Humber Arm, driving to the end of the road and the tiny fishing village of Lark Harbour. As in many seaside communities, a cemetery occupied a prominent position overlooking the harbour. Tombstones faced the water in honour of those who perished at sea. While walking along the narrow main street, we noticed an array of codfish drying over circular baskets beside a small house. Two men, a father and son, were standing nearby so we introduced ourselves, asking first about the cod. An hour later, after detailing the salting and drying process, they discussed the plight of fishermen in these parts.

The father, retired Coast Guard, had fished out of Lark Harbour long before there was even a road here. He proudly showed us his sturdy and brightly painted orange dory, its flat bottom designed for surfing onto the beach with a following sea. "Da drick," he said, "was to get high and dry, before da surge sucks ya back."

He and his son ventured more than ten miles off shore, often in rough seas, searching for the increasingly elusive codfish. Other local fishermen did the same, some never returning.

As on Prince Edward Island, lobster fishermen here weren't getting enough money for their catch, just over three dollars a pound. According to the father, distributors and stores were profiting, not the fishermen. His son, who also owned a lobster boat, had to work winters at Alberta's oil sands to make ends meet. I asked how the cod fishing was since the '92 Moratorium controlled catch limits.

The father bemoaned, "Aulful. Da seals, sharks, and whales are eatin' all da cod dere is in deese wadders."

We expressed sympathy for their situation, thanked them profusely, and departed with a new appreciation for the hard work and dangers involved in offshore fishing. And if we ever caught any cod in the future, we'd know how to salt and dry them.

A short drive and a half-hour hike up a well-marked trail to Cedar Cove gave us time to reflect on our brief visit, vis-à-vis our earlier visit with a farmer in Saskatchewan. Although their routines were distinctly different and a country apart, a common thread of endless toil and unceasing dedication to a way of life passed down through generations bonded them together just as surely as if they were next-door neighbours. Elly enjoyed the hike, especially near the end where she lapped up the cool, clear waters of a spring-fed lake. Fresh moose prints in the mud heightened our awareness that we were not alone.

So, what sort of animal would have such big feet? she asked me.

"Do you remember back in Moose Jaw the animal that greeted us at the Information Centre?"

Oh yeah...let's move on.

A short distance away through a green meadow was an expansive bay, cradled by steep headlands. Knee-high boulders served as perches for us to sit and gaze at the shimmering sea, contemplating how fortunate we were to be traveling across such a beautiful country. As on so many other occasions, we felt proud to be Canadian. Juicy red raspberries, within arms reach of the trail, provided a tasty snack on our return hike.

Driving a short distance, we pulled into Blow Me Down Provincial Park to check its suitability for our big rig. Nope. Even the overflow area at the beach wouldn't have been wide enough for us to turn around. While there, we climbed a seemingly endless staircase up to an observation platform from which we could see the harbour far below: the small village, orange dory, and our fishermen friends still keeping a watchful eye on their cod. Before starting down, we bet dinner on who could guess closest to the actual number of steps. Sandy chose 450; I chose 400. We counted 422, slightly closer to my guess. Over dinner, she accused me of counting on the way up!

Our next couple of days was spent at a campground near Deer Lake, allowing me time to golf and Sandy time to just relax, maybe read; maybe not. When traveling and sightseeing for weeks on end, Sandy needs a day or two "just to veg out." I don't. Never have. I need to be doing something, preferably something physically challenging. I enjoy exercise of any kind: give me a pile of logs to split or a mountain to climb and I'm a happy camper.

That evening, we built the one and only campfire of our trip. Both Buster and Elly were suitably relaxed, having seen many campfires over the years. Simone, tense and wide eyed, was enthralled by the tiny sparks floating upward and disappearing into the night sky. As the fire smoldered, she cuddled into Sandy's sweater and stared at the glowing embers. What could she be thinking? Were the flickering flames causing primeval urges of fight or flight? Or maybe she was just enjoying the moment, like me, without a sustained thought in the world.

We toasted marshmallows and sipped hot chocolate, a ritual that campers everywhere have shared for decades. Not too many years ago, firewood was free in Canada. Today, most campgrounds charge by the bundle, some limiting fires to a communal pit. I'm guessing within a few generations campfires will be banned, the argument being that increasingly scarce wood should be used for products, not for burning. Although such a prohibition will take some joy out of camping, we'll hopefully think back to how irresponsible it was to burn wood at our campsites just to feel heat and stare blankly at glowing embers. Eventually we'll adapt, just as we have to wearing seatbelts in cars and not smoking in public places.

We still hadn't decided whether to haul the trailer 300 kilometres up the Viking Trail to the tip of the Northern Peninsula. Some RVers advised against the 4-hour trip because of steep hills and narrow roads, suggesting we park the trailer at a campground along the way then drive the remaining couple of hours in the truck. Some of these folks stayed overnight in motels to make the trip worthwhile since it takes at least a couple of days to adequately explore this area.

Fortuitously, on the day of our departure we spoke to a lady who had lived up that way. She looked at our rig and said, "No problem; the steepest hills are in Gros Morne National Park. Once you get through the Park, the rest is easy."

Our powerful diesel engine handled most hills with ease, including those in the Park. We camped near Rocky Harbour, a small community outside of the Park's jurisdiction so we didn't have to pay a daily user fee. Parks Canada brochures boast that National Parks are protected and preserved for the enjoyment of all Canadians. Yet, a daily user fee is required to camp, walk a beach, or hike a trail within Park boundaries. Shouldn't the brochure state that Parks are protected and preserved for the enjoyment of those who can afford the $8 per person user fee? That would have amounted to $32 for our two-day visit, in addition to fees for the several Park attractions we visited.

One fine morning, we joined a popular 2-hour boat tour in Western Brook Pond, a deep fresh-water fiord surrounded by shear granite cliffs. The sun's rays glinted off ink-black water like diamonds as we motored slowly through the valley. Tourists lined the rails to capture that perfect photo of Nature in all her glory. The Tour Guide directed our attention to several waterfalls, a sandy bay, and rocky resemblances of the "Tin Man in the Wizard of Oz" and a "Man's face looking at the sky." He also mentioned that the high grassy plateau above the cliffs supports a herd of 500 caribou, which migrate across the lake ice every winter. I had always pictured these animals much further north, in places like the Yukon or Northwest Territories. Yet, here they were on roughly the same latitude as Winnipeg and Powell River.

Around every bend in the long slender lake, the view was more spectacular than the last. Fortunately, this pristine environment will remain intact for future generations, as no one with the exception of experienced hikers with proper documentation is permitted on the mountain trails. A five-day hike extends from the lake over the upper plateau back to the Visitor Centre at the Park's southern boundary. Four hardy young people with full packs disembarked at the far end of the lake. I wished them well, with a secret yearning to be tagging along. I get the same restless feeling whenever I see a group of bikers on the road or a cruising sailboat weighing anchor. Can a gypsy's roving spirit ever be completely satisfied? I think not.

On a boardwalk trail leading back to the parking lot, we saw our first moose, a female grazing peacefully at a respectable distance. Reportedly, 125,000 moose reside in Newfoundland with an estimated 5,000 in Gros Morne.

A signboard at the Park's entrance indicated that "24" had been hit by vehicles this year within the Park. Hundreds of collisions, many resulting in human fatalities or injuries, occur annually throughout the province. MOOSE signs are plentiful, warning motorists to slow down in areas of higher density.

We saw many of these magnificent animals during our visit, some beside the highway. Often, vehicles were parked on the shoulder with people outside taking close-up photos. Although these animals are typically docile and pay little attention to tourists, males during rutting season and females with young can display aggressive behaviour that would make the clueless photographers run for cover. Having seen many instances of aggressive behaviour displayed by elk and buffalo in Alberta's National Parks, I have no doubt moose would behave similarly in these parts.

That afternoon, we drove a short distance south to the bowels of the earth, literally. Near the terminus of Route 431 is one of the few places on earth where visitors can walk on mantel rock, normally found deep below the surface. "Tablelands," a mountain of orange brown rock thrust up by Teutonic forces eons ago, is a unique geological feature that earned the Park's designation as a UNESCO World Heritage Site. "It's a geologist's dream," stated one brochure. Not being a geologist, I never dream about rocks; maybe flora and fauna on occasion, but never rocks.

A half-hour hike to a viewing platform provided a panorama of the barren landscape, in contrast to the lush green mountain across the valley. Apparently, these sterile mineralized rocks are not conducive to plant growth; the few struggling shrubs in evidence were only knee high.

Based on her remarks, Elly didn't care for that walk either. *I never saw one feathered or furry animal the whole time; not even a rock that looked like a cat. I'm more like my dad...give me flora and fauna any day.*

That evening at a local tavern, we watched a 4-man display of Newfoundland music, culture, and humour, typically referred to as a "Kitchen Party" or "Time." Many of the audience participated in their rousing sing-a-longs, providing an atmosphere of good cheer that kept us smiling most of the night and half the next day. I was surprised at how many locals actually knew the words to the seafaring folk songs.

We broke camp around noon, just as it began to sprinkle. Heading north, our wipers moved at a slow even tempo, keeping pace with some of last night's musical ballads playing softly in my mind.

Within an hour, light sprinkles had turned to a deluge and a grey mist shrouded the landscape on both sides of the road. The wipers were now slapping lively and my attention was focused on the yellow line.

We had planned to stay at a seaside campground near Port au Chois, about halfway to the Meadows, but after viewing the site in driving wind and rain, I chose instead to continue. "Earl," a Force 3 hurricane, was reportedly somewhere out in the Atlantic headed in our direction. In the event he decided to arrive that evening, I didn't want to be camped on a beach.

As it turned out, Earl stayed at sea for another week and then made a direct hit on Halifax, Nova Scotia. Although we were some 800 kilometres away, we still felt some of his wrath in strong wind and rain. Little did we know that we would soon face a more direct onslaught of another monster being spawned in the Tropics.

As the maelstrom continued, we crept through seaside towns with ominous names like "Deadmans Cove" and "Savage Cove." Nearing our destination, I detected a thin sliver of bright sky low on the distant horizon. Gradually, the sliver expanded and the dark clouds lifted like a new day dawning.

The sun shone as I backed the trailer between clusters of white birch trees beside a chattering brook. Talk about a "Time" ... I was thinking more Titanic time!

The next morning, we drove the truck a short distance to L'Anse aux Meadows, site of the first Viking settlement in North America. Parks Canada's Visitor Centre provides displays outlining events that occurred here a thousand years ago, 500 years before Columbus and Cabot. Reportedly, Leif Erikson (son of Erik the Red) sailed from Greenland to Newfoundland and established a small settlement on this grassy meadow. Leif's sister Freydis led two subsequent expeditions to this same location.

Shortly thereafter, the settlement was abandoned partly for economic reasons and partly because of conflicts with resident Beothuk Indians. Archeologists discovered the site in 1960 and spent the next ten years unraveling its mysteries.

A Parks Canada tour guide, who participated in those archeological digs, showed us where several of their original sod huts had once stood. Only rock foundations bulging beneath protective grass covering were evident.

Various Viking artifacts such as iron boat nails, a stone oil lamp, and a bronze pin, together with ancient sagas from Norse literature, validated the time and location of this settlement. Replica sod huts complete with costumed interpreters made this UNESCO World Heritage Site come alive.

Sod hut at L'Anse aux Meadows, Newfoundland

During our travels up the coast, we had noticed more than a few flags, vertically striped white, pink, and green, flying from homes and businesses. The white represents Scotland, pink England, and green Ireland, countries that contributed to the cultural mosaic of Atlantic Canada. This flag represented Newfoundland and Labrador prior to their joining Confederation in 1949. "Dese," said one local responding to our question, "are flags of da Newfoundland Republic."

Apparently, many Newfies still feel that the province is a Republic, officially part of Canada but separate from it, both geographically and politically. "We're not as radical as Quebec Separatists, but consider ourselves different dan most Canadians."

Sandy asked a staff person at Lanse'aux Meadows, "Do you consider yourself a Canadian first or a Newfoundlander first?"

He replied, "No question, ma'am, I'm a Newfie first. After all, Canada didn't join us 'til 1949." We all chuckled.

During the next few weeks, we asked that same question of more than a dozen locals. Almost all said that they were Newfies first. One recently retired gentleman, after much deliberation, said, "Oh, I'm about 'alf and 'alf and it varies from day to day."

His major gripe about being Canadian was the cost of traveling on the ferry, to and from the mainland. "Da ferry should be an exdension of da Drans-Canada. Why should I ave to pay to dravel dat part of da 'ighway, just cause id's over wadder?"

I replied, "Good point. Your argument strikes a cord with those of us in British Columbia that rely on ferries."

"And anoder ding," he said, "I'm not 'appy with da way we're ignored by Ottawa just cause we're out 'ere in da middle of da ocean." He said some other things about the "rich, fat-ass cats" in Ontario and Alberta, which led me to assume that at least on this particular day, he was feeling more like a "Newfie first."

At the tip of the Northern Peninsula, a ferry crosses the Strait of Belle Isle to Quebec near the southeast corner of Labrador. We decided not to visit Labrador, a mostly barren and sparsely populated part of the province of Newfoundland and Labrador (abbreviated, NL).

To put it another way, of these two separate land areas that form one province, we only visited Newfoundland. The capital of both is St. Johns but each has their own Ode, songs that capture the essence of these interrelated but separated lands.

On our map of Canada, I was amazed to see that the province of Quebec, which we had left over a month ago, cradles the triangular-shaped Labrador, bordering the entire southern and western edges. The eastern edge is bordered by the Labrador Sea. About 500,000 people reside in NL, 150,000 in St. Johns, with most of the remainder scattered about in seaside communities or along the Trans-Canada Highway. We would spend the next few weeks visiting some of these communities, mostly located on small peninsulas that jut out into the Atlantic Ocean on Newfoundland's east coast.

After our tour of the Meadows, we dined at a local restaurant that served caribou burgers. Like our friend Jo back in British Columbia, I'll try almost anything at least once. Not surprisingly, they tasted like hamburger.

Later in our trip, I would also eat scrunchions and cod tongues. The former are pieces of deep-fried hog rinds that crunch when chewed and taste like chunks of pigskin. The unique texture of cod tongues took some getting used to, deep-fried on the outside with a jelly-like centre. Even while eating them, I wasn't convinced that codfish actually have tongues. Later, in a fish market I peeked inside a cod's mouth. Sure enough, they do have tongues, which led me to wonder about their evolutionary value since to my knowledge no other fish have them.

On our return trip down the west coast, we camped one night near Cow's Head in order to visit nearby Shallow Bay, which has one of the few white sandy beaches in Newfoundland. A few others are scattered along the east coast.

Returning to Deer Lake, we headed east on the TCH halfway across the province to Grand Falls-Windsor. We dry camped at a shopping centre there.

August 30th was Buster's 13th birthday so we had a proper party, sticking a candle in a can of tuna and singing "Happy Birthday." Elly howled along enthusiastically. Buster didn't care about the singing or his new stuffed mouse. He just wanted tuna. We taught him good manners by sharing with Simone and Elly.

Newfoundland's coasts are dominated by fishing, the interior by forestry and mining. Along the highway, we saw heavily forested hills to distant horizons with occasional lakes and rock-cuts similar to northern Ontario. Even the graffiti was similar: JAMIE + CAROL spray-painted inside a heart-shaped border.

The next morning we pulled into to a campground at Lewisport, unhitched and drove on Road to the Isles which terminates at Crow Head lighthouse, one of the few manned lighthouses in Canada. Although this location is ideal for spotting icebergs and whales, we saw neither. Earlier in the year, even during the summer, bergs pushed south by the Labrador Current are visible along most of the east coast of Newfoundland while humpback, minke, and fin whales migrate through these waters on their way to the St. Lawrence River.

Twillingate is a pristine community, "even the air smells fresher," according to one CFA (Come From Away) who encouraged us to visit. We hiked up a trail TOP OF TWILLINGATE, which wasn't one of Elly's favourites. Her feet kept slipping through gaps between the boards on sections of the wooden stairs. *If you want me to join you on this walk, you'll have to carry me.* She can be demanding at times.

With the occasional carry, we reached the platform at the top, which offered panoramic views of Twillingate Island. But the best part of our hike was picking wild blueberries on the way down.

Sandy's mom loved to pick berries for pies, jams, and muffins. Sandy seems to have inherited Rhena's berry-picking genes. She picked and picked, intent on filling a plastic shopping bag. Berry picking in Newfoundland is very popular in late August, early September. Pickers were everywhere filling buckets with abandon. Other sought-after berries, each with their ecological niche, include Crow, Partridge, and Crabapple. Fortunately, we never found their niches or Sandy would still be picking.

On our drive back to the campground, we saw a sign by the road advertising a dockside seafood restaurant. Pulling into the parking lot and not seeing a restaurant, I asked a local where it was. "Just walk between those two buildings," he said.

We did, and, sure enough, tables and folding chairs were set up on a floating dock with a water view. The waitress told us they had already sold out of lobster but their other specialty was snow crab, which several other patrons seemed to be enjoying. When it arrived with the various dissecting tools, I remembered why I normally don't order crab. I dislike the feeling, which I often got in my college anatomy classes, of cutting into a cadaver that may have been someone's mother. If not for the garlic butter, it wouldn't be worth the effort. I made a mental note to add crab to the list of things I'll never ever order again: fried clams, caribou burgers, scrunchions, and cod tongues.

From Lewisport, we drove southeast to the Bonavista Peninsula where we camped for several days. Sandy had called the campground near Charleston a few days earlier to make a reservation for the Labor Day weekend. When the gentleman said they were full, Sandy suggested we would call back in a couple of days to see if there was a cancellation.

"You do that girl," was the man's reply. Sandy had been called "girl" several times since we arrived in Newfoundland, perhaps one of the reasons she enjoyed her visit so much.

We did manage to get into the overflow section of the campground which, being on the shore of a small lake, actually turned out to be more scenic than the serviced section. Discovery Trail meandered through several quaint fishing villages to the town of Bonavista.

It was near here where John Cabot presumably landed in 1497 and claimed this "New Founde Lande" for England. Scholars still debate the exact landing site, but a bronze stature of the explorer is located on a rocky headland at Bonavista.

After a visit to an historic lighthouse, we toured a full-scale replica of Cabot's ship "Mathew," floating in Bonavista Harbour. It has a length of 80 feet, weight of 50 tons, and reportedly carried a crew of 19 on the historic voyage. Our guide mentioned that a similar ship built in Bristol, England had re-created Cabot's 34-day crossing, arriving in Bonavista on June 24th, 1997. A celebration of the 500th anniversary of the historic landing was well attended, including Queen Elizabeth and other dignitaries.

On our return trip down the peninsula we stopped at nearby Elliston, a small town known as the "Root Cellar Capital of the World." According to their brochure, the oldest cellar was built in 1839, the newest in the 1950's. Forty-two of these structures have been restored. Originally used to store fish and locally grown root vegetables—cabbage, potatoes, and radishes—today they stand empty but bear testament to the ingenuity and perseverance of Elliston's early settlers.

The provincial bird of Newfoundland and Labrador is the Atlantic Puffin. Looking much like a small parrot with a red bill and webbed feet, they nest in the summer months on islands near the coast. One nesting site is a small grassy island just a stone's throw from Elliston.

Unfortunately, the puffins seen there a week earlier had already departed for their wintering grounds in the north Atlantic. Imagine how incredibly hardy these birds must be to spend their winters at sea, diving down 100 metres in freezing waters to catch fish and squid! It seems appropriate that they should be the provincial bird, symbolic of the hardy souls that inhabit these rocky shores. The only puffins we saw were in craft shops adorning calendars, pottery, jewelry, and postcards.

The next day, we hiked Skerwink Trail named after the shearwater, a seabird that lives mainly offshore. This five-kilometre trail near Trinity East, in our opinion the most scenic in Canada, follows the coastline on craggy cliffs along Trinity Bay.

Elly enjoying the view from Skerwink Trail, Newfoundland

Huge granite structures project skyward from the water just offshore. Boardwalks, which Elly negotiated with ease, lead through bogs and pristine meadows. Split-log steps notched into steep hills lead to magnificent seascapes and back down through primordial forests. Ferns, algae covered rocks, mushrooms, and moss-draped trees provided a surreal feeling.

Two brown rabbits got Elly's attention. I reminded her to "just watch" as she stood rigidly, every fibre of her being wanting to move closer, staring at the little fur balls until they bounded off into the forest. *Well, that was exciting!*

In the ocean swells below a precipitous drop-off, we spotted a dead moose that obviously hadn't read the sign CAUTION, STEEP CLIFFS. Time to put Elly on leash.

Somewhere between the two and three kilometre markers, we looked out upon a picture postcard view that will be forever etched in my memory: a century-old lighthouse in the harbour with the enchanting village of Trinity on the far shore. A low crimson sun added to the ambience, reminding us that this would not be a good place to be after dark.

Breaking our trance, we hustled the final two kilometres to the parking lot just as the last remnants of daylight departed.

Each year, Rising Tide Theatre in Trinity presents a diverse range of original productions that capture the essence of the province's rich history and unique culture. That evening, we delighted in the sights and sounds of "Brand New Beat," a rollicking musical based on a popular TV show during the 60's in Newfoundland: The Art Andrews Dance Party. Great fun! Great talent!

The next day we attended another production, The New Founde Lande Trinity Pageant, which depicted life in this historic community from the 1500's to the 1800's. Elly walked with us through winding streets and alleys as costumed actors portrayed an array of colourful characters. She delighted the crowd at the outset by howling along to the singing of "Ode to Newfoundland."

The tour guide said that even if you were not a Newfie it was okay to sing the Ode, as long as you sang from the heart. *And so I did, which now makes me an honourary Newfie!*

Later, an actor referred to her as a "fine sheep." Everyone loved our little actress.

One scene was particularly heart wrenching: it referenced a seal hunt just offshore that turned tragic when the weather changed suddenly from calm and sunny to a bitterly cold gale, resulting in the deaths of twenty-four men and boys. We walked through a graveyard, then into a church where the audience served as congregation while a preacher tried to comfort "relatives and friends," mentioning each of the deceased by name.

Ten scenes, mostly of hardships, encouraged us to reflect on how our forefathers struggled to support their families and in the process to help build a nation. Sandy and I considered the Trinity experience one of the highlights of our trip.

Elly agreed: *I met two rabbits, led a sing-a-long, and portrayed a sheep, all in one day.*

Our next stop was Avalon Peninsula, its long slender finger sticking up between Trinity and Conception Bays. We camped in Brigus beside charming Hawthorne Cottage, home of Captain Bob Bartlett the skipper who took Peary to the North Pole in 1909. Various artifacts in the cottage, including a model of the sailing ship, reminded us of the courage required by such early explorers in their pursuit of discovery. I could just imagine setting sail with the likes of Erickson, Cabot, Cook, and Peary. Let's see, that would make me about 1,000 years old. But hey, why spoil a perfectly good image with a dose of reality?

From Brigus we drove to Cupids, the town where it all began, at least for the British. Four hundred years ago, in August 1610, Cupids was established as the first English colony in Canada. The French had already established a settlement five years earlier at Port Royal in Nova Scotia and three years earlier at Quebec City. Obviously, territorial claims were less important than military superiority; otherwise, Canada's primary language would be French. Only in New Brunswick is French considered one of the two official languages.

Just north of Cupids is Harbour Grace, another historic town. Sandy commented, "What a lovely name; wouldn't you like to tell people you live in Harbour Grace?"

"Not really, Powell River is lovely enough for me."

We stopped for a photo beside a bronze Amelia Earhart, the first woman to make a trans-Atlantic flight, May 20, 1932. A dirt road lead uphill to an unused airport, now a National Historic Site, where Amelia lifted off on her news-making flight to Paris.

Elly romped, rolled, and whizzed on the well-maintained grass strip, leaving her mark beside a legend of aviation.

A significant event occurred on the west shore of this peninsula at Heart's Content, another lovely name for a town. Incidentally, Heart's Desire and Heart's Delight are adjacent towns, but it was Heart's Content where the first trans-Atlantic telegraph cable was landed, in 1858, reaching along the bottom of the ocean to Valencia, Ireland.

Initially, I considered it odd that the cable was brought in on the west side of the peninsula rather than the east, which would be closer to Ireland. I learned later that this location was chosen because of its sheltered and relatively unused harbour.

Farther south along the peninsula at Hopeall, we stopped at an equine centre for our first look at the Newfoundland pony, an animal one size up from the Newfoundland dog.

These ponies had been inbred for 300 years, but according to the groomer, they are now on the decline, being no longer required for work. One of their ponies had just retired after 30 years of being a stud and stood by the rail, smiling, as the groomer brushed his main and applied a softening gel to his hooves.

Elly displayed her usual and sensible approach-avoidance behaviour with large four-footed animals: *I like to get close enough for a good sniff, but far enough away to avoid getting squashed.*

The Newfoundland dog was also bred for work, but today is more in demand as a house pet. Later, in St. John's we lingered at a monument dedicated to this lumbering, gentle giant and another dedicated to the Labrador Retriever, which actually originated in Newfoundland.

In 1894, the province commemorated a postage stamp with a picture of a Newfoundland, the first stamp to feature a dog. When I told Elly this, she commented: *I think France should have a stamp with a poodle on it.*

"I'll check, and let you know."

The one thing about Elly, and I suspect most dogs, her memory for holding me accountable is not all that great. It's unlikely she'll bring up the subject of French stamps again!

Moving down the forefinger and around to the thumb, we arrived at St. John's and were immediately inundated with mid-afternoon traffic coming at us from every direction. That big-city feeling came back with a rush, literally.

For several weeks, we had been visiting small villages where the pace would have suited Henry David Thoreau: slow and measured. Traffic was never an issue except on those occasions when two cars arrived at an intersection at the same time. If road rage in a small Canadian town were to occur, it would likely take the form: "You go." "No, you go." "I insist." "Please." "Hey buddy...."

Throughout our travels, we noted one axiom about Canadians that likely applies universally: politeness is inversely related to the size of a metropolis. People were noticeably friendlier in smaller towns.

That raises the question: does politeness transfer across settings? Do the manners of city folk improve when they find themselves temporarily in the country? Probably; otherwise, we would find impolite behaviour occurring in rural settings when city folks visit. We never saw a single incident of that phenomenon in all of our rural travels—everyone was polite.

We did, however, find more than a few ornery drivers among city dwellers. If setting does indeed shape the person, city folks might benefit by spending more time is small towns.

St. John's is not that big, only 150,000 people which is relatively small for a capital city. But its recent growth spurt, partly a result of offshore oil developments, seems to have outstripped its capability to transport people, similar to Fort McMurray in Alberta. No trains, no subways, just buses, cars, and trucks shuttling in and out of the city, congesting the narrow streets, many one-way, many under construction. To explore this vibrant city, we parked the trailer at a shopping centre for a few days and then relocated to a downtown campground for a few more days.

During most of our time in Newfoundland, the weather had been sunny and warm, a bit breezy at times, but wonderful for sightseeing. During our week in St. John's, it rained almost every day.

According to Environment Canada, St. John's is the wettest, foggiest, cloudiest, and windiest city in Canada. But the locals are proud of their climate, just as we were when living in Edmonton, calling it "character-building and invigorating."

We mentioned to a local man that a hurricane was expected to hit Newfoundland within the week. He quipped, "Good. Dat means we'll get a break from da windy wetter we bin havin." It didn't turn out quite the way he anticipated.

Sandy is very well organized, likely a result of her teacher training. She would peruse the brochures and booklets we had accumulated, highlighting attractions that either interested us or that we'd been told about. In or near St. John's, these included The Rooms, Signal Hill, Cabot Tower, Fort Amherst, George Street, Water Street, the Terry Fox Monument, and Cape Spear.

For the outdoor attractions, we waited for dry weather, which unfortunately coincided with the arrival of a huge cruise ship in St. John's Harbour, its 3000 passengers all wanting to visit these same attractions. And they did, by the busloads.

Elly got an obscene amount of attention from dog owners who were "missing their babies." Only a couple of people out of dozens knew her breed. Everyone enjoyed her attention and she's very good at attending to devotees as long as they're fussing over her. Of course, let a cat or some other furry creature catch her eye, and she would turn her back on a ham bone.

The Rooms was a "must see" attraction recommended by just about every visitor to St. John's. Located on a hilltop with a commanding view of the harbour, this modern museum with its steep roofs symbolizes a link with the past. In the early days when fishing reigned supreme, every seaside community had an array of steep-roofed buildings where families came together to process their catch. These "rooms," as they were called, were as central to a community as The Rooms is to the city of St. John's. Once the site of Britain's Fort Townshend, this facility offers "collections, exhibitions, and programs that tell our stories and interpret our natural world through art, artifacts, archaeology, architecture and archival records." We spent four hours browsing several floors of exhibits and could have stayed another four if they hadn't closed for the day.

Harbour at St. John's, Newfoundland viewed from Signal Hill

Signal Hill is reportedly St. John's most popular landmark and its status as a National Historic Site is well deserved. Towering high above the mouth of the harbour, it once served as a vantage point to signal the city below, by flag, as to the country of incoming vessels, allowing either defence or preparations for docking. Atop the hill is Cabot Tower, a massive stone structure that served as a focus for signaling since 1897. Nearby is the site where Marconi received the first trans-Atlantic wireless signal in 1901, holding his antenna aloft with a kite! From the tower we could look across the narrow entrance of the harbour and see the remnants of Fort Amherst, built by the British to protect the harbour.

Farther south along the coastline is the lighthouse at Cape Spear, the most easterly point in Canada. We drove there, hoping to wade into the ocean with Elly as a symbolic gesture of completing our cross-country journey, but that wasn't going to happen.

Crashing emerald-gilded waves and steep cliffs just beyond the viewing platform did not invite dipping, which suited Elly just fine. *Oh boy, oh boy ... I don't have to go swimming.*

At this point, we had crossed Canada from sea to sea, and our journey could well have ended. However, since we hadn't seen much of Nova Scotia or New Brunswick, we decided to spend more time revisiting these two provinces. But first, we had more to see in Newfoundland.

No matter how bad the weather, we were determined to visit Water Street, the oldest street in North America, and George Street, which reportedly has more pubs per metre than any other street in Canada. We walked the length of both in the rain, stopping occasionally to check out points of interest.

Just off Water Street, a small monument marks the spot where Terry Fox dipped his foot into the ocean before beginning his Marathon of Hope run on April 12, 1980. The plaque is just large enough to include a few significant dates and inspirational words. How fitting!

A local woman told us the city was planning to replace the diminutive monument with a grandiose statue, similar to the one we saw in Ontario where his run ended. A humble and shy young man, Terry would very likely be the first to suggest that any money designated for a fancy monument be used in the fight against cancer.

On George Street, we became honourary Newfoundlanders by participating in a "Screech In." This traditional ceremony involves reciting some maritime phrases, downing a shot of Screech, and kissing a cod on the lips. Screech is a Newfoundland brand of rum made in Jamaica, which according to our bartender, is still purchased from the Jamaicans in exchange for our codfish. He added, "That's my story and I'm sticking to it."

The ceremony, popular with tourists, was fun. Just for the record, though, there was no tongue involved during my kiss—by either party.

An elderly friend who had served in WWII suggested we visit the Crow's Nest on Water Street, a private club that he had frequented during the war. Memorabilia, including club logbooks, provided a glimpse into the lives of Canadian servicemen during the turbulent war years.

On the roof was a working periscope from a captured German submarine, U-69. This sub committed the last act of warfare in Canadian waters, sinking the SS Caribou in 1942 with a loss of 137 people as the passenger ship was crossing from North Sydney to Channel Port aux Basque. Coincidentally, we would return to North Sydney on the SV Caribou, a ferry named in memory of this ill-fated ship.

Leaving St. John's, we continued south through the village of Bauline East to a campground situated high above the ocean. When we arrived, the entire coast below was immersed in fog.

Slowly the sun burned off the grey shroud, revealing first the tops of several small islands, then lower and lower until we could see bands of incoming waves dashing against rocky shorelines. A series of craggy headlands receded to the far horizon. We spent some time relaxing in the campground's cliff-side gazebo, awed by yet another example of Canada's unbridled beauty.

A short distance to the south is the historic village of Ferryland. Established in 1621, it is reportedly the second oldest English settlement in New Founde Lande. Although we perused its history and ongoing archeological research, what we enjoyed most was lunch on a grassy bluff overlooking the ocean.

An historic lighthouse has been converted to a restaurant, specializing in picnic lunches: soup, sandwiches, and dessert packed in a wicker basket complete with a tartan blanket. Upon ordering, we were given a flag, in our case a Scottish flag, to distinguish us from other customers when our order was ready.

This practice was based on a centuries-old tradition of flags being used to identify merchant ships approaching St. John's harbour. The entire concept was ingenious, the food superb, and the setting spellbinding.

From our grassy knoll, a scene of natural splendour graced our table. Royal-blue water met robin-egg sky on the far horizon, waves crashed against rocks, sea gulls soared, and the pure, clean smell of sea delighted our senses.

Elly helped the dishwasher by licking our plates. *Dad even gave me a piece of his sandwich, which he never does, so I knew it had to be a special day.*

It was special, in a melancholy sort of way.

Sandy and Elly having a Lighthouse Picnic at Ferryland, Newfoundland

We had traveled east as far as we could go in Newfoundland. Tomorrow, we would return to the Trans-Canada Highway and begin heading back to the ferry, with one or two diversions along the way.

"Igor the Terrible" is what astronauts were calling a monster hurricane churning about in the Caribbean. As a Category 4, he passed by Jamaica causing extensive damage, then continued offshore up the eastern seaboard. Within a week, he was projected to be nearing the south shore of Newfoundland, downgraded to a Category 1. Our plan was to be well inland on the day of his arrival. We had two days to make our way to a campground on the Eastport Peninsula and another day to explore the charming seaside community of Salvage, "one of the oldest continuously inhabited settlements in North America." The day Igor was expected to reach Newfoundland, September 21st, we had planned to get up early and drive an additional 70 km further north, out of harm's way. That was the plan.

Rain and wind startled me awake at 6 am. "Igor's here," I said to Sandy, "and he's not happy." We weren't going anywhere, at least by choice. By 11 am, the wind had increased to 100 kph, gusting to 140 kph. Rain and leaves were blowing horizontally. I brought in our three slides to reduce surface area and reattached the truck for more weight. Several adjacent trailers were blown about, bending their support jacks at useless angles. The wind prevented taking Elly outside before dinner. At 40 pounds, she would have been bowled over. I nearly was when I struggled to put an extra wheel chock under our neighbour's unoccupied trailer, which threatened to relocate. She was probably too scared to pee anyway. *"Petrified" might be a better word. The noise was deafening; the floor shimmied. But I can still pee when I'm petrified, so Dad's plan may not have been the best option. But I was a good girl and waited, and waited, and waited.*

For six hours, we hunkered down in the rocking trailer with trepidation, concerned that some nearby trees might land on us. Being on-edge for that length of time was emotionally draining. Sandy coped by going to bed where she managed to read, snooze, and teach Elly, who had snuggled in beside her, about "denial." By late afternoon, electricity and water had been knocked out in the campground. We piled on an extra blanket that evening as the wind continued to howl.

The next morning, the wind had died down to a stiff breeze while sunshine glinted through puffy white clouds. The campground looked like a war zone: tree branches and debris scattered everywhere, trees uprooted, satellite dishes knocked over, and RV awnings ripped or blown away. Both of our vehicles, normally gleaming white, were speckled with leaf fragments. Our heavy wooden picnic table was flipped over; a neighbour's tool shed relocated. A large Y-shaped elm next to us had split down the middle, both trunks swaying precariously. The buzz of chain saws filled the air. People clustered in small groups discussing the damages, partly I suspect to alleviate anxiety with a collective sigh of relief. Survival in traumatic situations builds bonds between those similarly affected.

Folks who had listened to media reports knew that roads and bridges in large areas along the east coast were washed out, isolating communities and stranding travelers. Some houses had flooded; others were washed away. Only one fatality was reported: an elderly man, checking on his neighbour's property, was washed away with rubble when a driveway collapsed. Many power lines were down, water supplies cut off, and even the Trans Canada Highway was closed in two locations, one just west of our campground: "Closed indefinitely until damages could be assessed."

Our forced delay allowed us to do some grocery shopping in the small town of Eastport. Comfort food was at the top of Sandy's list. Fortunately, one store had used a generator to keep their freezer operating so they still had ice cream. A local newspaper described the destruction as worse than word on the street. Reporters labeled it the "Storm of the Century" and "Canada's Katrina," the most powerful and devastating storm ever to hit Newfoundland. "Tens of millions of dollars in damages," according to Premier Williams. "I've never seen damage like this before anywhere in Canada," said Prime Minister Harper, following his tour of the hardest hit areas. Everyone rallied together, sharing food, water, and shelter to those in need. Governments, the military, businesses, and volunteers helped provide supplies and services to affected communities. "Returning to normal" was expected to take at least a year.

Two days later, traffic was allowed back on the Trans-Canada, so we made our way to Gander. At the town's Information Centre, the receptionist informed us that Igor had stranded hundreds of travelers, all accommodated in town. Gander and surrounding communities already had a reputation for accommodating stranded travelers. On 9-11 when many US-bound planes were diverted to Gander airport, over 10,000 passengers were billeted in homes, schools, and lodges for days, demonstrating once again Canadian's willingness to offer a helping hand to those in need.

In Gander, we visited the Silent Witness Memorial commemorating the 256 people who died in a horrific plane crash, the worse in Canada. Nearly all of the fatalities were members of the 101st Airborne Division, returning to Fort Campbell, Kentucky in 1985 after a peacekeeping mission on the Sinai Peninsula. They had stopped at the Gander airfield on a cold December morning to refuel. Shortly after take off, their plane crashed, presumably because of a build up of ice on the wings. The memorial includes a plaque of the names and rank of each person who perished as well as a bronze statue of an American soldier holding the hands of two children, each grasping an olive branch to signify the peacekeeping nature of the mission. The silent witnesses are the natural surroundings at the crash site: trees, hills, and rocks overlooking Gander Lake.

From Gander, we drove west to Deer Lake for one night, then south to Codroy Valley, passing through the potentially dangerous Wreckhouse, again without incident. From a nearby campground, we visited Codroy's harbour. As sailors, we always seemed to find a harbour when near the water. A group of fishermen were busy unloading their catch and sorting by size, tasks to them as mindless as breathing. In answer to our questions, we learned that one boat had caught 2,000 pounds of fish since four o'clock that morning; that the limit, per license, is 3,000 pounds per week but that some boats had two licenses, allowing them to double their quota; and that they would do it all over again tomorrow, and the day after, as long as it took to reach their quota.

According to one fisherman, when Newfoundlanders talk about "fish," they are referring to cod. All other species are referred to by name, such as "salmon." He told us that commercial fishermen are not permitted to catch salmon and that all Atlantic salmon available in local markets is farm grown. Unfortunately, open-pen salmon farming creates the same problems here as in British Columbia: wild salmon in close proximity to the pens become infected with lice, decimating survival rates. The obvious solution, which was already occurring on a small scale in BC, is to raise farm salmon in self-contained pens, isolated from wild salmon.

The real problem of fishermen here, as we'd heard elsewhere, had nothing to do with salmon or lice; it had to do with the low prices for cod and lobster. Even several years ago, cod and lobster were worth twice as much. "Des days, I can 'ardly make enough to feed me family." When I asked this fisherman how long he had been fishing for a living, he replied, "too long." Another disgruntled fisherman said he would never encourage his children to fish for a living: "my son makes $8,000 for tree weeks work in Alberta's oil fields, more dan he would make all fall fishin 'ere."

I raised the issue of whether their Fisherman's Union could do more to regulate prices. "Ah, dem Unions, all dey want is our money. Dah dree big distributors," holding up his knurly fist and raising each of three fingers sequentially, " in Newfoundland, Nova Scotia and PEI, are God; dey set dah prices to increase der profits." Not one fisherman we met wanted to fish for a living; they continued out of necessity. There were no other jobs, nor could they sell their boats or equipment. When I asked about the future of fishermen in Newfoundland, one man remarked, "Like da once almighty cod, dare a dyin' breed."

After five centuries of drastically over-harvesting, the seemingly boundless fish stocks were nearly depleted and a tradition of living-off-the-sea was vanishing. I wondered whether we might use this lesson to ensure it doesn't happen with other natural resources such as coal, oil, and wood, all of which are being depleted at an alarming rate. Sadly, I suspect this scenario will reoccur ... only the casualties will differ.

The next morning we departed this wonderful province with heavy hearts: sad to be leaving, and concerned for the hospitable fishermen and their families we were leaving behind. Steinbeck fell in love with Montana, "its grandeur and warmth." We felt similarly towards Newfoundland, especially its people. If we were allowed to revisit only one province, it would be the Rock, hurricanes and all.

11
NOVA SCOTIA (continued)

From the ferry terminal at North Sydney, we drove a short distance into the country, noting a marked difference in the landscape between our August departure and late September arrival: the deciduous trees had changed from lush green to glorious shades of burnished red, gold, and yellow. Fall had made its mark and we were the benefactors.

From our campground on Cape Breton Island, we visited the nearby Fortress of Louisbourg. Our tour guide described the difference between a "fort" and a "fortress," the former was used for military purposes only while the latter included a functioning town within fortified walls. The French built this fortress in the early 1700's to protect their fishing rights on the nearby Grand Banks. Louisbourg became the capitol of the regions settled by the French, at that time Cape Breton Island and Prince Edward Island. After a couple of sieges over as many years, the British took possession of the Fortress. Soon after, they destroyed the buildings and rock walls to prevent re-occupation by the French. Today, this National Historic Site, containing more than 50 restored buildings, is the largest reconstructed 18th Century town in North America. Costumed interpreters portraying soldiers, merchants, and servants provided an entertaining and informative glimpse of life in 1744 when the fortified town was still occupied by the French.

Our travels in the Maritimes made us painfully aware of how often France and England battled for territorial rights in Canada: at Montreal, Quebec City, St. John's, Louisbourg, and many other locations. I found it difficult to remember who won which battle when. Sometimes the French won, sometimes the British. To simplify matters, I chose 1763 — the year the Seven-Year War ended with the signing of the Treaty of Paris. From that year onward, British sovereignty ruled in Atlantic Canada with the exception of two small islands off the southern coast of Newfoundland, St-Pierre and Miquelon. These were proclaimed French territories and remain so today. Consequently, visiting France from Canada involves just a short ferry ride.

Following our visit to Louisbourg, we returned to Sydney for a night at a local shopping mall before setting out for Halifax. It was October 1st, Elly's 11th birthday so we celebrated by sticking a candle in a beef bone and singing happy birthday. Elly howled along, her nose pointing toward the ceiling, her tail just a wagging. After blowing out the candle, Elly commented, *I don't feel 77!* "And you certainly don't look it," I said, never expecting her medical diagnosis that was just a few weeks off.

Leaving Sydney, our route took us first along the south shore of Bras d'Or Lake, across the Canso Causeway, and onto Marine Drive, 325 kilometres of scenic, but mostly rough roadway along the eastern shore beside the Atlantic Ocean. At the upper reaches of Country Harbour, this route funneled us onto a ferry, costing $5 per vehicle regardless of size. Our rig took up most of the loading deck. Only one car joined us, driven by a couple from Austria who had spent the past two weeks touring Nova Scotia. They were nearing the end of their holiday and openly envied our lifestyle: not having to count the days when lives would go back to ordinary.

Shortly after disembarking we camped for an evening, still a couple of hours drive from Halifax. Our next campground was near Peggy's Cove, a name that comes to many people's minds whenever "Nova Scotia" is mentioned. I had always imagined it to be on the coast, far removed and desolate. It is on the coast, but only a half-hour west of the thriving metropolis of Halifax. For me, visiting Peggy's Cove was a deja vu experience. I was sure I'd already seen this cozy little harbour with its century-old lighthouse, smooth granite rocks, colourful boats, and weathered fish shacks. Of course, I had...in paintings and on postcards, calendars, and magazine covers. Artists from around the world flock to this little hamlet with brushes and cameras, attempting to capture the essence of what might be the most scenic square kilometre in the world. The Austrian tourist we had met on the ferry, whose camera lens was the length of a bazooka, told me he took over a thousand photos here in just one afternoon. Charm oozes from every crevice in this rugged, serene village, "not-to-be-missed" for every visitor to Nova Scotia.

Peggy's Cove, Nova Scotia

A humorous quip about seniors is that some are reluctant to buy green bananas, not sure if they will live long enough to see them ripen. Not of that ilk, a 70-year-old retired art instructor from Peggy's Cove embarked on an ambitious ten-year project to transform a granite rock in his backyard, the size of a school bus, into a monument to honour local fishermen. Beginning in 1977, William deGarthe, using power tools and hand chisels, crafted over two-dozen life-size images of hard-working fishermen and their wives. Also included are a guardian angel and an image of Peggy, a young girl who supposedly was the only survivor of a local shipwreck and after whom the Cove is named. Unfortunately, deGarthe passed away in 1983, leaving his "labour of love" only partially completed but inspiring to all who view it.

We spent a few days in Halifax and were impressed by its harbour, one of the largest in the world. Ferries, tour boats, and pleasure craft shuttled about while tankers came and went from Dartmouth's refineries across the harbour. Most of Canada's naval ships are stationed here although a number were reportedly in Newfoundland assisting with the aftermath of Igor. At least one large cruise ship was in port every day of our visit, contributing to an onslaught of tourists at the various attractions.

About a million people reside in this capital city, creating an excessive amount of traffic on its narrow, one-way streets that crisscross its steep hills. We signed up for an amphibian tour bus, which introduced us to the city's major attractions and ended with a splash into the harbour for a mariner's view of the city. Among other things, our tour guide pointed out two large office buildings at water's edge built on circular columns, which transfer cold seawater up into the building for cooling purposes, an environmentally friendly and economical method of air-conditioning.

On the basis of our guide's suggestions, we visited several attractions in the downtown area. Most tourists visit the Citadel, an English fort that occupies a prominent position overlooking the harbour. Completed in 1865 to defend Halifax against an attack by the United States, the fort never come under siege; consequently, it was vacated by the British in 1906, the date of withdrawal of all British forces from Canada. During both World Wars, it was used as a command centre and to house troops going overseas, a major staging area for naval activities in the North Atlantic. Formally known as Fort George, it was proclaimed a National Historic Site of Canada because of its role in shaping Canada's history. Having recently been to other forts and fortresses, we chose to forgo a visit, opting instead to tour a brewery.

October 5th was Alexander Keith's 215th birthday. Party posters were everywhere, inviting people to join in celebrating the occasion. Keith emigrated from Scotland to Canada at 22 years of age and established a brewing company in Halifax. The year was 1820 and good beer was hard to come by. Since sailors and soldiers were allotted a daily quota of beer, a ready market was available. And because Keith took great pride in making good beer, his brewery prospered. This astute businessman also became a politician, serving as Mayor of Halifax for three terms. We learned all this and more during our tour of Keith's brewery. Costumed interpreters provided a lighthearted presentation in the techniques of early beer making, as well as a couple of mugs of Keith's finest. But we did more than drink beer in Halifax.

The Museum of the Atlantic provides exhibits related to Nova Scotia's involvement in seafaring activities; its collection of artifacts is one of the largest in Canada. A permanent exhibit on the Titanic and Halifax's involvement in the recovery of victims was especially informative. The Titanic had 2200 passengers and crew aboard when it collided with an iceberg on April 14, 1912—over 1500 perished. Most of the 705 survivors were firstclass passengers, taken to New York by the nearby liner Carpathia. Halifax, being the closest port to the ill-fated ship, sent three vessels to recover over 300 bodies: 150 were returned to Halifax to be buried in three different cemeteries. As was the case with the survivors, most of the bodies returned were first-class passengers. According to our tour guide, "The rich-and-famous continued to receive priority even after death. The owners of the Titanic were concerned about lawsuits from influential relatives of first-class passengers who had perished. They were less concerned about lawsuits from relatives of crew and third-class passengers who were provided burials at sea."

Five years after the Titanic sank, Halifax harbour was the scene of an even greater maritime disaster. On a December morning in 1917 the Mount-Blanc, a French cargo ship with tons of wartime explosives aboard, accidentally collided with another vessel. The disabled ship in flames slowly drifted toward a pier as many spectators gathered on shore, watching in astonishment. That's when it happened...a massive explosion destroyed two square kilometres of Halifax, killing 2000, and injuring another 9000. This disaster is still considered the world's largest accidental man-made explosion. Only atomic bombs have killed and injured more people, albeit not by accident.

Another interesting exhibit, especially for boaters, identified over 10,000 shipwrecks off the coast of Nova Scotia. The highest concentration is at Sable Island, a treacherous sandbar 300 kilometres southeast of Halifax. Over 350 ships, the first in 1583, have floundered in this "Graveyard of the Atlantic." In the late 1800's, five lifesaving stations were established along the 44-kilometre length of the island. Many shipwrecked sailors were rescued and cared for in manned shelters until they could be transported to Halifax. Because of improved navigational equipment, only one small yacht has run aground here since 1947. This exhibit also displays artifacts recovered from various shipwrecks in Atlantic waters: silverware, anchors, dishes, buttons, coins, and even a wooden deck chair from the Titanic, the only one in existence.

All this mayhem occurring on ships had me thinking that perhaps flying might be a safer means of transportation ... until we stopped by a memorial near Peggy's Cove. On September 2, 1998, Swissair Flight 111 with

229 people aboard crashed into the ocean eight kilometres southwest of Halifax. Everyone perished. Boats from Halifax and nearby fishing communities had the gruesome task of recovering bodies, or more accurately, pieces of bodies that were later identified through dental records, fingerprints, and DNA testing. Even today, some people involved with the recovery efforts are continuing to receive post-traumatic-stress counseling.

Our little Simone turned six months of age in Halifax, an age when kittens can be spayed. We had the operation done in a cat hospital and stayed at our campground an extra two days to ensure there were no complications. Knowing she was fine, we relocated further west to Lunenburg for a few nights. Why Lunenburg? Because the famous Bluenose schooner has a berth in Lunenburg and we wanted to learn more about this majestic Canadian icon, images of which are imprinted on Nova Scotia license plates and Canadian dimes. At the Fisheries Museum of the Atlantic, we learned why the Bluenose became so famous.

Sailing schooners were becoming increasingly popular in the late 1800's. With two masts and fore-and-aft sails, they were fast, maneuverable, and could carry heavy loads, suitable for offshore fishing. Occasionally, they would race informally to and from the Grand Banks. Apparently, many of the captains of these vessels were appalled at the ideal conditions required by America Cup racing yachts. In 1919, the New York Yacht Club cancelled the America Cup race because of 23-knot winds, considered a stiff breeze by hearty schooner sailors. Discussion began on an alternative international racing series involving working schooners. It seemed like a good idea since there was already a friendly rivalry between the United States and Canadian boats whenever two of them were on the same patch of ocean. Most sailors who read this will be able to relate to that observation. So, in 1920 an International Fishermen's Trophy race was scheduled to determine the fastest fishing schooner between these two countries. The Halifax Herald newspaper offered a prize of $6,000 and a silver trophy to the winner.

That first year, a schooner from Massachusetts beat the Nova Scotia entry and took the trophy to New England. To be more competitive, Lunenburg shipwrights built the Bluenose in 1921, to be used for fishing as well as racing. As the fastest Canadian schooner, she was entered in the international competition that year and won. She continued to beat every competitor in the United States for the next 17 years, until 1938, when the races were discontinued because there was no worthy competitor to challenge the Canadian entry.

The sad part of this story is that the Bluenose, when no longer needed for racing, was sold to a West Indies company that used her to haul freight. In 1946, she ran aground on a reef in Haiti and sank, an ignominious ending to a legendary sailing vessel that brought fame to Nova Scotia and Canada. In 1963, Bluenose II was built in Lunenburg for use as a tourist attraction and ambassador of Nova Scotia, often sailing to other ports on the eastern seaboard. At the time of our visit, she was undergoing a major restoration in a closed shipyard; however, we did see silver trophies awarded to the original Bluenose, tributes to the shipwrights who built her and the fishermen who sailed her.

At the Fisheries Museum, our guide used live lobsters to explain how to get the freshest lobster when selecting them from a tank. Since lobsters are not fed in holding tanks, they will occasionally eat the antennae of other lobsters. "Always select a lobster that has intact antennae since they are the most recent arrivals, thus the freshest."

The narrow, hilly, and one-way streets of Lunenburg were reminiscent of St John's and Halifax while the brightly coloured heritage buildings and seafaring ambience transported us back in time to the 19th Century. As a classic example of British colonial planning, Lunenburg was declared a UNESCO World Heritage Site.

Lunenburg Harbour, Nova Scotia

A short distance north is Mahone Bay, another attractive seaside community. We arrived during their annual Scarecrow Festival, which added to the fun atmosphere. Nearly every store displayed scarecrows depicting such characters as the royal family, cast of Gilligan's Island, legends of rock and roll, Phantom of the Opera, and many pirates. We spent an afternoon perusing galleries and specialty shops along the waterfront. Elly joined us and got the usual admiration from many of the passer-bys. One elderly grey-haired lady asked what colour she was. "Well, she used to be chocolate brown. But during the past few years, she's added some grey, which makes her look more mature and sophisticated, don't you think?" I knew she'd agree. "Of course, she's lovely," was her reply, giving Elly a few gentle pats.

Elly had been very healthy for all of her eleven years. Annual vet appointments involved routine shots and check ups. But during the past few days, a disturbing behaviour began: without even knowing it, she was urinating in her bed and while lying on the carpet. She gave us furtive guilty looks when we cleaned up her messes. "That's okay Elly, it's not your fault," was our standard reply. At a nearby clinic, the vet diagnosed her problem as "Incontinence," which he said, "is not uncommon with older spayed females, especially those that were spayed prior to coming into heat," which Elly was. He prescribed a medication to increase estrogen levels and said we should see an improvement within a week. Fortunately, the medication together with limited access to water prior to bedtime and frequent opportunities to "go outside" allowed her to be dry throughout the night. Within several weeks, she no longer needed the medication or water restrictions, which had me questioning whether her condition might have been more related to a bladder infection.

Regardless of the cause, we were relieved that our precious Miss Elly was back to her old self. Interestingly, Steinbeck's Charley also got sick about halfway through their trip — a distended abdomen — requiring a visit to a vet. He too became his old self after Steinbeck administered some pills "to flush out his kidneys." Perhaps these two traveling canines were kindred spirits in more than just breed.

While living in Edmonton, I taught boating courses for the Canadian Power and Sail Squadron. When discussing tides, I always referenced the Bay of Fundy for having the highest tides in the world. The tidal range, from low to high tide, on the coast of BC is around 10 to 15 feet, while in the Bay of Fundy it's around 40 to 50 feet, the height of a four-story building. "Imagine," I would tell my students, "anchoring in a bay in 6 feet of water and putting out 40 feet of anchor rode, sufficient for the depth. Six hours later, your rode is straight down and your anchor is off the bottom." I used this example to illustrate the importance of knowing the local tidal range and allowing sufficient rode for high tide.

A "tidal bore" is the rush of water that occurs as the tide rises in confined spaces such as a riverbed entering the Bay of Fundy. The seawater pushing upstream actually reverses the flow of water, often with a substantial advancing wave. I was looking forward to seeing the effects of these large tidal ranges when we got to the Bay of Fundy in a day or two.

After leaving Lunenburg, we drove west along the shore to Liverpool. Here, a friend agreed to receive some forwarded mail from another friend who regularly emptied our PO Box in Powell River. Dry camping for a night at a nearby community hall allowed us to catch up on the past five years since we last met at a wedding of Sandy's Godson in Vancouver.

On October 15th, the date many Canadian campgrounds close for the winter, we left the scenic south shore and drove a couple of hours north to one of a scattered few campgrounds that stayed open until the end of October. Our site overlooked the Bay of Fundy, giving us a close up view of this natural wonder. Twice a day, a reported 100 billion tons of seawater rush into the shallow bay, piling up until the force of gravity pulls it back into the deeper ocean. Since lobster season had just begun in Nova Scotia, only a few boats were in a nearby marina. In the early evening, these boats could be accessed from the dock, floating in 30 feet of water. At noon the next day, they were sitting on the bottom, their dock lines hanging straight down. To my amazement, all the water was gone. Deep keel sailboats would not do well in these marinas, nor did I see any.

We were told to try the scallops in Digby, "Scallop Capital of the World," so we drove into town half expecting to see a giant fibreglass scallop. There was none to be seen except the pan-fried varieties sautéed in white wine and butter sauce, which were excellent. The next day, a local lobster fisherman said, "Digby has the best tasting lobster in the world." I couldn't let that pass without verification so I picked up a freshly cooked lobster and got out my dissecting tools. After a half hour of cracking and picking, I concluded that they are tasty, but how would I know if they are the best in the world? But even if they are, getting at the meat is hardly worth the effort in my opinion. I added whole lobster to my growing list of never-eat-again foods.

The next morning, we drove east to the Exhibition Grounds in Windsor, the closest campsite to the town of Grand Pré (pronounced "Grand

Pray"). Here, in an expansive meadow was one of the largest Acadian settlements prior to the Deportation. Although the Visitor Centre of this National Historic Site of Canada had closed for the season, we walked the well-kept grounds, which included a church and blacksmith shop. Signposts described communal activities, while bronze statues embodied the dreams and heartaches that occurred in this rural setting during those tumultuous years.

Our next stop was a campground near the small town of Truro where we were able to observe a tidal bore on the Salmon River. This twice-daily event was scheduled to occur at 10:45 the next morning. We arrived at the viewing site a half-hour early, joining a dozen other spectators on the riverbank, not knowing what to expect. Would a wall of water rush up river with a roar, inundating everything in its path? Two women positioned themselves lower down close to the water with cameras in hand and then reconsidered, joining the rest of us on an upper bank. One candidly expressed her concern, "We didn't want to be swept away." None of us had ever witnessed a tidal bore so we waited with anticipation, and to be frank, some trepidation.

Laughter erupted when it finally arrived. Apparently, the advancing wave can range from a few centimetres to a metre in height, depending on the height of tide. That morning, the bore appeared as a small ripple slowly and quietly making its way upstream. Within a half hour, the river had changed its direction of flow but the effect was considerably undramatic to say the least. Someone suggested coming back in a week during full moon when the bore would be … well, less boring.

Thirty years ago, beautiful large elms lined the streets of nearby Truro. Since then, Dutch Elm disease killed them. Rather than cut the trees down completely, town council wisely chose to retain the substantial trunks on which wood carvers could sculpt significant people in the town's history. On such sculpture depicted Vera Clyke playing the organ, which she had done in the same church for 71 years until her death in 1998. Using a guided street map, we viewed several dozen other sculptures of people, from politicians and business owners to volunteers and musicians. Who would have thought that dead tree stumps and an abundance of artistic ability could provide such a memorable glimpse into Truro's heritage?

12

NEW BRUNSWICK (continued)

Leaving the "Tree Sculpture Capital of Nova Scotia," we headed west on the first toll road of our trip, making good time on this four-lane highway. Crossing the border into New Brunswick, we soon entered the thriving metropolis of Moncton, unfortunately during rush-hour traffic. After seemingly endless jostling, we finally exited onto a less congested road, heading south to a campground on the Bay of Fundy. Hopewell Rocks, a popular tourist attraction, was closed for the season, but we could still access the beach to see these spectacular geological structures.

We went first at low tide, descending a four-story staircase to the ocean floor. At first Elly was reluctant to walk on the iron-grated steps, but a guiding hand on her collar helped her along. *If only Dad's eyes were as close to the steps as mine, he would see that there is nothing below us but a four-story drop to the ocean floor.*

Huge limestone structures resembling flowerpots, sides eroded and tops covered in grasses and trees, were randomly positioned about the beach, as were tunnels and caves carved by eons of rising and falling tides. I asked a lady from Alberta, who had also been visiting the eastern provinces, what she enjoyed most about the Maritimes. She looked up and said, "These monoliths. They are absolutely magnificent." A dozen tourists were taking photos from every conceivable angle to try and capture the grandeur of these structures. As usual, my photos were an injustice to Mother Nature's stupendous works of art.

With the tide out, we were able to walk a half-kilometre to the water on a gravel beach. Incidentally, I should point out that technically tides don't go in and out; they go up and down. But either way, you get my drift—oops, bad choice of words.

Elly at Hopewell Rocks, New Brunswick

The next day with the tide in (up?), 35 feet of water covered the area where we had been walking yesterday. The lady's comment made me consider whether such "freaks of Nature," as Steinbeck would have called these unique structures, add to Canada's identity as a country. After all, they *are* only rocks and could have just as easily been located in another part of the world. I suppose one could say that for other natural wonders such as the Rockies, Niagara Falls, Northern Shield, Lake Superior, Gros Morne...

Move these to other parts of the world, and Canada becomes...well, not quite Canada. No, I would argue that such marvelous natural icons as well as man-made ones contribute to making this a unique and wondrous country. To quote the lady: "Absolutely magnificent."

We drove into Moncton and neighbouring Dieppe one day to shop and again joined throngs of people heading home from work. Another day, we drove south to Cape Enrage to see what some photographer described as "The best view in Canada." Waves crashing on the reefs below a lighthouse with the sun setting behind a cloud bank provided a spectacular view. But I could show him even better views if he came with me to Newfoundland. Without a doubt, Canada has more great scenery than anyone's memory can retain, but the view of Trinity from the Skerwink Trail tops my list, with the seascapes in Ferryland and Bauline East a close second. To gain a canine's perspective, I asked Elly what her favourite scenery was during our travels: *Cats would top my list, with cows and rabbits a close second.*

We wanted to visit St. John farther west along the Bay of Fundy but couldn't find a campground open. So, we drove to the capital city of Fredericton and camped along the Saint John River for what we thought would be a few days. The weather was spotty, raining one day, sunny the next. I managed to get in a round of golf at a local course that was shutting down the next weekend. In retrospect, I had golfed in every province except Manitoba, and my game hadn't improved one iota. Is a lesson in order?

Buster and Simone gazing at the Saint John River in
Fredericton, New Brunswick

On Saturday, we visited the weekly Farmer's Market. Crowds of shoppers shuttled from booth to booth, inside and outside, purchasing fresh meats and vegetables, jewelry, purses, jams, and various lunch items from fast-food booths. A busy place indeed, but fortunately, it closed at 1 pm or Sandy would have spent the afternoon there. One vendor, who sold photographs, told us about a scenic route down to Saint John, with a few ferry rides across the river. We planned to spend Monday exploring this route, but some serious rain cancelled that idea. Instead, we drove around Fredericton, visiting several old churches, all of which were closed.

The perception of time passing, quickly or slowly, depends on what is happening in your life. If you're in a distressing situation, perhaps in a hurricane or at the dentist, time passes slowly; an hour can feel like a day. However, if you're engrossed in something you enjoy—your favourite hobby or meeting with friends—the hours pass quickly. It seemed like only yesterday that we were saying goodbye to our friends in Powell River, and here we were, over two years later, nearing the end of our journey.

Our plan was to leave on Tuesday if a package had arrived by courier. Our satellite dish was knocked down and broken by Igor so I ordered another from the cable company to be sent to Fredericton. Unfortunately, it didn't arrive until Wednesday so we planned to leave on Thursday. That plan was also cancelled when Sandy woke up feeling "under the weather." It reminded me that I should get my annual flu shot, which I did at a local clinic, no charge. While I was getting my shot, Sandy went to another clinic for a checkup and was prescribed medication by a doctor, no charge. Our health care system is another thing I like about Canada. Each province has its own medical plan, but all residents have access to health care, wherever they may be in Canada. That's not to say we don't pay, in some provinces like BC we do—a monthly fee covers most of our medical needs in other provinces. Private medical insurance for out-of-country travel is available, and it's advisable to purchase a plan before leaving the country. The cost of health care in other countries such as the United States has financially ruined many uninsured Canadians. We plan not to be among that group.

We stayed yet another day, and it was now late October. The recently colourful leaves had fallen, leaving naked limbs reaching into crisp autumn air. New Brunswick's landscape, together with much of Canada, was changing from green to brown in preparation for winter. Halloween was just around the corner, thus the decorative displays of goblins, witches, and pumpkins in shops and on residents' porches. Subfreezing temperatures and brisk winds penetrated the trailer, prompting our baseboard heaters to run constantly. After two days, Sandy was feeling well enough to travel so we headed for the US border, just an hour west of Fredericton.

Along the way, we stopped in the town of Nackawic to see "The Worlds Largest Axe." Its blade contains seven tons of stainless steel and its handle angles upwards 15 meters, a tribute to the many loggers in New Brunswick who helped build a promise land in the wilderness.

Nearing the end of his journey, Steinbeck became road weary to the extent that he stopped observing. His "search for America" had actually ended several states before he returned home, as it had for Charley who "carried out his functions like a sleepwalker." We, on the other hand, were already discussing a plan to do a similar journey in reverse, east to west, without traveling the same route.

This country is so much larger than I had envisioned—the second largest in the world after Russia—and we had only traveled a small sliver along the southern border. It's understandable why the name "Canada" is derived from a native word meaning "Big Village." It's also more beautiful than I could have imagined, with landscapes and seascapes that defy description. But most of all, it was the people—the friendly and hospitable folks—that made our journey so enjoyable, and that help to define who we are as a country. Wherever we went throughout the ten provinces, we felt welcomed and justifiably proud to be Canadian.

Although I had fulfilled my objective of gaining a better understanding of Canada, I must confess that Canada's geographical, historical, and cultural complexity cannot be captured in a single narrative of observations gathered along roadways. Maybe, just maybe, if we complete a return trip, I'll have more than scratched the surface of this glorious land I call home.

I asked Elly what she liked best about her travels across Canada. With tilted head, joyful eyes, and wagging tail, she replied: *Just being with family, having fun!*

Select MSI Books

Animal Books

Christmas at the Mission: A Cat's View of Catholic Customs and Beliefs (Sula)

Easter at the Mission: A Cat's Observation of the Paschal Mystery (Sula)

How My Cat Made Me a Better Man (Feig)

Intrepid: Fearless Immigrant from Jordan to America (Leaver & Leaver)

Noah's New Puppy (Rice with Henderson)

Saints I Know (Sula)

Sula and the Franciscan Sisters (Sula)

Tale of a Mission Cat (Sula)

Culture

Arabic in a Hurry (Farraj)

Road to Damascus (E. Imady)

Russian in a Hurry (Leaver)

Syrian Folktales (M. Imady)

The Rise and Fall of Muslim Civil Society (O. Imady)

The Subversive Utopia: Louis Kahn and the Question of National Jewish Style in Jerusalem (Sakr)

Thoughts without a Title (Henderson)

When You're Shoved from the Right, Look to Your Left (O. Imady)

SELF-HELP BOOKS

100 Tips and Tools for Managing Chronic Illness (Charnas)

A Woman's Guide to Self-Nurturing (Romer)

Creative Aging: A Baby Boomer's Guide to Successful Living (Vassili-adis & Romer)

Divorced! Survival Techniques for Singles over Forty (Romer)

Helping the Disabled Veteran (Romer)

How to Get Happy and Stay That Way: Practical Techniques for Putting Joy into Your Life (Romer)

How to Live from Your Heart (Hucknall) (Book of the Year Finalist)

Life after Losing a Child (Young & Romer)

Publishing for Smarties: Finding a Publisher (Ham)

Recovering from Domestic Violence, Abuse, and Stalking (Romer)

RV Oopsies (MacDonald)

The Widower's Guide to a New Life (Romer)

Widow: A Survival Guide for the First Year (Romer)

Widow: How to Survive (and Thrive!) in Your 2d, 3d, and 4th Years (Romer)

www.ingramcontent.com/pod-product-compliance
Lightning Source LLC
Chambersburg PA
CBHW052007090426
42741CB00008B/1588